STEP-BY-STEP
Irresistible Chocolate

STEP-BY-STEP

Irresistible Chocolate

Elizabeth Wolf-Cohen

Photography by Edward Allwright

SMITHMARK

This edition published in 1994 by
SMITHMARK Publishers Inc.,
a division of US Media Holdings Inc.,
16 East 32nd Street
New York
NY 10016

SMITHMARK books are available for bulk purchase for sales
promotion and for premium use. For details write or call the
Manager of Special Sales, SMITHMARK Publishers Inc.
16 East 32nd Street, New York, 10016; (212) 532–6600

Produced by Anness Publishing Limited
1 Boundary Row
London SE1 8HP

ISBN 0 8317 7842 3

Editorial Publisher: Joanna Lorenz
Series Editor: Lindsay Porter
Editor: Gillian Haslam
Designer: Peter Laws
Jacket Designer: Peter Butler
Photographer: Edward Allwright
Stylist: Maria Kelly

10 9 8 7 6 5 4 3

Printed & bound in Hong Kong

CONTENTS

INTRODUCTION

Chocolate, one of the world's most beloved foods, is enjoying an all-time popularity. It is an ingredient with a long and impressive pedigree: for centuries the Aztecs drank a bitter, frothy drink called 'chocolatl', made of roasted cocoa beans mixed with water or wine. Cocoa beans were then introduced to Europe in the sixteenth century, and cocoa became a food of kings. Its true potential was not exploited until the early nineteenth century when the chocolate press was invented in Holland, but from that point onwards, chocolate has gone from strength to strength. It is now available in countless forms and varieties, and is used as a flavoring in every conceivable dessert and sweet – bitter chocolate is even used in some savory dishes.

This book is for all lovers of chocolate. It contains a glorious array of fabulous desserts and sweet indulgences – cakes, pies, tortes, mousses, ice creams, cookies, brownies, muffins and truffles galore – using chocolate in every guise. The recipes are special enough to share with friends, or give as gifts, but be sure to make an extra batch to enjoy yourself – they are truly irresistible.

Types of Chocolate

Chocolate is found in many different forms, ranging from solid to pre-melted, from extra dark to white, from unsweetened to sweet and milky. All chocolates, even those of the same type, taste different, depending on the quality and roasting of the cocoa beans, the quality and style of production and the national tastes of the country where the chocolate has been manufactured.

Eating and cooking chocolates are made from chocolate liquor which is blended with extra cocoa butter, sugar and flavorings. The more chocolate liquor (mass or solids) and butterfat the chocolate contains, the higher the quality. Although certain types of chocolate lend themselves to certain preparations, chocolate is very much a personal preference.

Chocolate chips

Originally produced by chocolate manufacturers for use in chocolate chip cookies, these pieces are available in various sizes and as bittersweet, semi-sweet, milk and white. Because they are designed to keep their shape in a variety of baked goods, they are best used in recipes like cookies, cakes and confections. Although they can be melted, they contain less cocoa butter than ordinary chocolate.

Cocoa

Cocoa is the pure chocolate mass which is left when the cocoa butter has been removed from the chocolate liquor. Ground and sifted, cocoa gives the most intense chocolate flavor to baked goods and desserts.

Dutch-processed cocoa or Dutch cocoa is neutralized by a process called 'Dutching', giving the cocoa a darker, reddish color but a slightly milder flavor. This is sometimes called European-style cocoa, as almost all imported cocoas are Dutch-processed or 'natural'.

cocoa

Non-alkalized cocoa which is commonly available in the US has a sharper flavor because the acids are left untreated. Unless specified, the two types can be interchanged although the flavor of 'natural' cocoa will be more intense. In baking, cocoa should be sifted into the dry ingredients or diluted with boiling water to form a paste, much like cornstarch, before being added to other mixtures.

Drinking chocolate or other hot or cold chocolate commercial preparations are made from cocoa to which sugar and sometimes dried milk solids have been added.

Couverture or covering chocolate

This is a very fine, richly-flavored chocolate which has a high proportion of cocoa butter, giving it a glossy appearance and smooth fluid texture. It is expensive and mostly used by professionals for coating and dipping other chocolates. This chocolate must be 'tempered' (see page 12). It is available in some speciality shops or by mail order as bittersweet, semi-sweet, milk or white chocolate.

Although it can be used when a very fine flavor and texture are required, it is not generally used in baking or desserts. Do not confuse couverture with commercial coating chocolate or cake covering, made with the addition of other fats and oils, which are cheaper and easier to use, but lack the flavor and gloss of fine couverture.

chocolate chips

couverture chocolate

dark chocolate

unsweetened chocolate

Milk chocolate

Milk chocolate is made with dried milk powder. It has a much milder, more creamy flavor than dark chocolate and cannot be substituted for bittersweet or dark chocolate in baking and dessert recipes because it has a lower cocoa solid content. Extra care should be taken when melting it.

Dark, bittersweet and semi-sweet chocolate

These types of chocolate contain only chocolate liquor, cocoa butter and sometimes lecithin (an emulsifier), sugar and vanilla in varying quantities. Each country has different guidelines for the content of cocoa solids, which accounts for the wide variety in quality. In the US chocolate must contain 34% solids and in the UK 35%. Best results in cooking are obtained with chocolate which contains a minimum of 50% chocolate solids. The recipes specify one of these types, but you may substitute one type for another and use, for example, a more bitter chocolate if you prefer a less sweet flavor.

Unsweetened chocolate

Also known as 'Bakers' chocolate' or 'bitter' chocolate (not bittersweet), unsweetened chocolate is the cooled chocolate liquor blended with a quantity of cocoa butter. It contains no sugar, has a bitter, full chocolate flavor and is used mainly in manufacturing chocolate products. For baking, an adequate substitute for 1 oz unsweetened chocolate is 3 tbsp cocoa plus 1 tbsp unsalted butter. The sugar in the recipe must also be adjusted according to the recipe.

White chocolate

Technically, white chocolate is not chocolate at all because it contains no chocolate liquor. It is a commercial product made from cocoa butter, milk and sugar. It is technically called a confectionery coating and some white chocolate may contain vegetable fat as well as, or instead of, cocoa butter, so read the label carefully. White chocolate has recently become very popular and is used in mousses, cakes and sauces and as a contrast to other chocolates. As with milk chocolate, it is sensitive to heat, so be very careful when melting it. Use a bain marie or water bath and keep the temperature between 225–250°F.

milk chocolate

white chocolate

Equipment

The only chocolate work requiring specialized equipment is molding. Other equipment can be improvised.

Cake tester
A thin metal skewer used for testing cakes.

Chocolate molds
Available in many shapes, plastic molds are easy to use.

Chocolate tools
The triangle and dipping fork are used for coating chocolates and truffles. A kitchen fork can be used.

Cookie sheets
Heavy duty, non-stick cookie sheets make baking easier.

Cutters
A selection of different shaped cutters is useful.

Double boiler
Useful for melting chocolate and cooking custards.

Ice cream scoop
A small scoop is ideal for biscuit mixtures and truffles.

Instant-read thermometers
Very useful in chocolate and sugar work.

Marble slab
Provides a cold surface for pastry and chocolate work.

Measuring spoons
Essential for accurate measuring of ingredients.

Metal spatula
A metal spatula is useful for removing goods from cookie sheets, spreading creams and fillings.

Pastry bag and tips
A selection is essential for decorating and piping.

Spring-form pans
Used to make desserts which cannot be inverted for unmolding. The clip-on side forms a tight seal.

Sugar thermometer
Used to measure high temperatures when cooking sugar.

Swivel-bladed peeler
Used for peeling fruits, removing citrus zest and making chocolate curls.

Tart pans
Choose a good quality metal pan with a removable bottom for easy unmolding.

Wooden skewers
Used for testing cakes and moving delicate ingredients such as chocolate curls.

double boiler

flour dredger

sieves

swivel-bladed peeler

metal spatula

kitchen knife

kitchen plates

chopping board

pastry bag and tips

kitchen scissors

marble slab

sugar
thermometer

measuring
cup

wooden
spoon

cook's
knife

cutters

measuring spoons

chocolate
molds

instant-read
thermometer

cake tester

rubber
scraper

spring-form
pans

tart
pans

mixing
bowls

electric
mixer

KENWOOD

wire
rack

chocolate
tools

wooden
skewers

ice cream
scoop

cookie
sheet

Choosing and Storing Chocolate

Before buying chocolate, check the recipe and use what the recipe calls for; always buy the best quality of its type.

In general, all chocolate should be kept in its original wrapper if possible, or wrapped in foil and then plastic. Store in a cool, dry place at about 65°F. High humidity will shorten the shelflife of chocolate. Do not store chocolate in the refrigerator. Unsweetened and dark chocolates will keep for years in ideal conditions. Milk chocolate will keep up to a year, and white chocolate, because of its high butterfat content, will keep for 6–8 months. Certain chocolates, such as couverture and bittersweet chocolate, as well as prepared chocolates, freeze well.

Incorrectly stored chocolate will 'bloom'. 'Sugar bloom' occurs when chocolate is exposed to moisture. As the moisture evaporates, it draws out tiny particles of sugar, leaving the surface looking 'moldy'. 'Fat bloom' occurs when the chocolate has become too warm. The cocoa butter begins to melt and forms grayish-white areas on the surface.

Although unattractive, bloom does not affect the flavor and the chocolate can still be used.

Cooking with Chocolate

If chocolate is being melted alone, all the equipment must be *completely dry* as water may cause the chocolate to thicken and become a stiff paste. For this reason, do not cover chocolate during or after melting it as condensation could form. If chocolate does thicken, add a little pure white vegetable fat (not butter or margarine) and mix well. If it does not work, start again. Do not discard chocolate: it may be used in a recipe where the chocolate is melted in another liquid.

Chocolate can be melted with a liquid, but there must be sufficient liquid. If melted with butter, cream, milk, water, coffee or a liquid that is unlikely to burn, generally 1 tbsp of liquid to each 2 oz of chocolate should be safe, but if the chocolate appears to be thickening, add more liquid.

With or without liquid, chocolate should be melted *very slowly*. It is easily burned or scorched and overheated chocolate can turn gritty and develop a poor flavor. Dark chocolate should not be heated above 120°F. Milk and white chocolates should not be heated above 110°F.

Tempering Chocolate

Tempering is the process of gently heating and cooling chocolate to stabilize the emulsification of cocoa solids and butterfat. This technique is generally used by professionals with couverture chocolate, which allows the chocolate to shrink quickly (to allow easy release from a mold, for example with Easter eggs) or to be kept at room temperature for several weeks or months without losing its crispness and shiny surface. All solid chocolate is tempered in production, but once melted loses its 'temper' and must be re-tempered unless it is to be used immediately.

Untempered chocolate tends to 'bloom' or becomes dull and streaky or takes on a cloudy appearance. This can be avoided if melted chocolate is refrigerated immediately as chilling the chocolate solidifies the cocoa butter and prevents it from rising to the surface or 'blooming'. General baking and dessert-making do not require tempering, which is a relatively fussy procedure and takes practice. However, it is useful when preparing sophisticated decorations, molded chocolates or coatings. Most shapes can be made without tempering if they are refrigerated immediately.

1 Melt the couverture chocolate by the preferred method – the microwave method is quick, easy and the least messy. The temperature should be about 110°F. Stir to be sure the chocolate is completely melted and smooth.

2 Pour about three-quarters on to a marble slab or cookie sheet and, using a metal spatula or plastic scraper, quickly scrape into a pool in the center and then spread out again. Work the chocolate for 3–5 minutes until no streaks remain. Scrape back into the chocolate remaining in the bowl and stir until blended. The temperature should be about 90°F. The chocolate is now tempered.

Double Boiler Method

This is probably the most traditional method of melting chocolate.

1 If you do not have a double boiler, place a small heatproof bowl over a saucepan. Make sure the bowl fits snugly so no water or steam can splash into it. Do not allow the water in the bottom of the double boiler or saucepan to come to a boil.

2 Place the broken or chopped chocolate in the double boiler top or bowl and place over double boiler bottom or saucepan. Lower the heat as much as possible, or turn it off completely, and allow the chocolate to melt slowly, stirring frequently.

Direct Heat Method

When a recipe directs melting chocolate with a liquid such as milk, cream or even butter, it can be done over direct heat in a saucepan.

1 Choose a heavy-bottomed saucepan and melt the chocolate and liquid over low heat, stirring frequently, until chocolate is melted and smooth. Remove from heat immediately. This method is also used for making sauces, frostings and some candies.

2 Chocolate can also be melted in a very low oven (about 225°F). Put the chocolate in an ovenproof bowl and place in the oven for a few minutes. Remove the chocolate before it is completely melted and stir until smooth.

Microwave Method

The microwave is ideal for melting chocolate quickly and easily, but remember to check it during the cooking time.

1 Place chopped or broken chocolate in a microwave-safe bowl and microwave on MEDIUM power (50%) for about 2 minutes for 4 oz bittersweet or semi-sweet chocolate. Milk and white chocolate should be melted on LOW power (30%) for about 2 minutes for 4 oz of chocolate.

2 These times are for a 650–700 W oven and are *approximate* times as both chocolate and microwave ovens vary, so check the chocolate about halfway through cooking time. The chocolate does not change shape, but begins to look shiny and must then be stirred until completely melted and smooth.

BE CAREFUL

Chocolate can burn in the microwave, so be sure to check frequently and continue to microwave at 5–10 second intervals if chocolate has not melted sufficiently.

Chocolate melted with liquid or butter may melt more quickly if the liquid has a high fat content, so check the chocolate frequently.

Grated Chocolate

Chocolate can be grated by hand or in a food processor. Make sure you grate it at the correct temperature.

1 Chill the chocolate and hold it with a piece of folded paper towel to prevent the heat of your hand melting it. Hold a hand or box grater over a large plate and grate the amount of chocolate required.

2 A food processor fitted with the metal blade can also be used to grate chocolate, but be sure the chocolate is soft enough to be pierced with a sharp knife. Cut the chocolate into small pieces and with the machine running, drop the chocolate pieces through the feed tube until grated. This produces very fine shavings. Alternatively, use the grater attachment and pusher to feed the chocolate through the processor for larger shavings.

Coating with Chocolate

Truffles, caramels and other candies, as well as fresh or dried fruit pieces, can all be coated in chocolate. Tempered couverture chocolate is the ideal method, but melted bittersweet or semi-sweet chocolate can be used if the chocolate is refrigerated immediately.

Solid Easter Eggs

To fill 4 egg shells, melt 16 oz of chocolate. Couverture chocolate should be tempered. Decorate the eggs with ribbon or colored foil.

1 To prepare the egg shell, pierce a hole in each end and blow out the contents into a bowl. Using a small pastry nozzle or skewer, enlarge the hole in one end, wash out the shell and leave to dry completely. Leave in a warm oven which has been turned off, or dry gently with a hair dryer; the shells must be completely dry before filling.

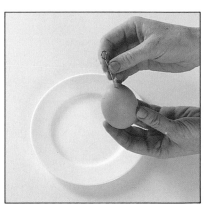

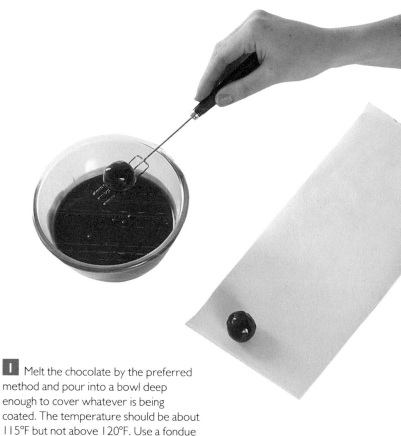

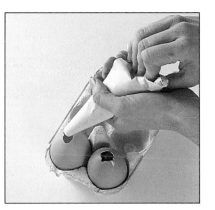

1 Melt the chocolate by the preferred method and pour into a bowl deep enough to cover whatever is being coated. The temperature should be about 115°F but not above 120°F. Use a fondue fork, skewer or special chocolate dipping fork to lower the sweet into the chocolate. Turn to coat completely and lift out of the melted chocolate, tapping gently on the edge of the bowl to remove excess chocolate.

2 Place on a waxed paper-lined cookie sheet, and if you like, draw the tines of the dipping fork across the top, lifting lightly to leave two raised ridges.

2 Cover the smaller hole with tape and place in an egg carton. Snip one corner of a paper cone and fit it with a small plain piping tip. Fill with melted chocolate. Insert the tip into the egg and slowly force chocolate into the shell, pulling the tip out as the egg is filled. Set overnight.

3 To take the shell from the chocolate, gently crack and peel off. Avoid touching the eggs with fingers as they leave prints. If shells are difficult to remove, freeze eggs for 1 hour and try again. Wrap each egg in colored foil or tie with ribbon.

Quick Chocolate Curls

Chocolate curls make an ideal decoration for many desserts and cakes, whether they are made from chocolate or other flavors. These curls can be made very quickly using a vegetable peeler, and can be stored for several weeks in an airtight container.

1 Bring a thick piece or bar of chocolate to room temperature (chocolate that is too cold will 'grate' and too warm will slice). With a swivel vegetable peeler held over a plate or cookie sheet, pull the blade firmly along the edge of the chocolate and allow curls to fall onto the plate or cookie sheet in a single layer.

2 Use a skewer or toothpick to transfer curls to the dessert or cake, as fingers will melt the curls.

Chunky Chocolate Curls

These curls are best made with dark chocolate which is melted with vegetable fat (about 1 teaspoon per 1 oz of chocolate), which keeps the chocolate from hardening completely.

1 Melt 6 oz bittersweet or semi-sweet chocolate with 2 tbsp pure white vegetable fat, stirring until smooth. Pour into a small rectangular or square pan lined with foil or waxed paper to produce a block about 1 in thick. Refrigerate until the chocolate is set.

2 Allow the block to come to room temperature, remove from the pan, then use a swivel peeler to produce short chunky curls, or grate as desired.

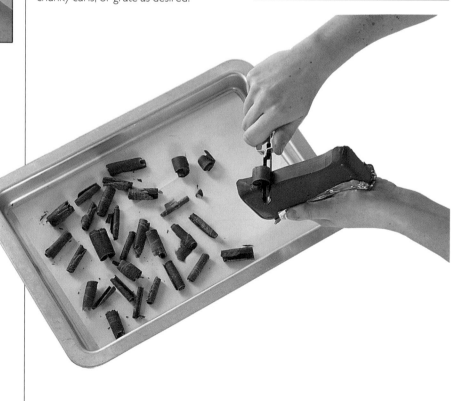

Chocolate Scrolls or Short Round Curls

Temper dark or white chocolate, or use chocolate prepared for Chunky Chocolate Curls to produce these scrolls.

1 Pour prepared chocolate on to a marble slab or the back of a cookie sheet. Using a metal spatula, spread to about ⅛ in thick and allow to set until just firm, about 30 minutes.

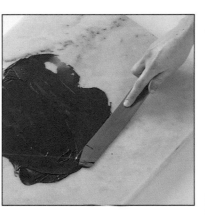

2 To make long scrolls, use the blade of a long, sharp knife on the surface of the chocolate and, with both hands, push away from your body at a 25–45° angle to scrape off a thin layer of chocolate. Twist the handle of the knife about a quarter of a circle to make a slightly wider scroll. To make shorter 'cup-shaped' curls, use a teaspoon to scrape the chocolate away.

3 A variety of shapes and sizes can be produced, depending on the temperature of the chocolate and the tool used to scrape the chocolate. Metal spatulas, paint scrapers, tablespoons and even a wide, straight pastry scraper can be used. The colder the chocolate, the more it will splinter; warm chocolate will give a softer, looser curl, but do not allow chocolate to become too soft or warm or it will be difficult to handle and may bloom.

Chocolate Shapes

These are easy to prepare with melted chocolate, and are ideal for decorating gâteaux or desserts.

1 Prepare melted chocolate and pour on to a waxed paper-lined cookie sheet and spread evenly to about ⅛ in thick. Allow to cool for 30 minutes or until firm. Invert the chocolate on to another sheet of waxed paper and, using a sharp knife and straight edge, trim edges to make a perfect rectangle.

2 Using the straight edge, mark even squares, rectangles or diamond shapes and cut with a knife.

3 Alternatively, use small metal cookie cutters to make a variety of decorative shapes.

4 Use a plain pastry tip to punch a hole in the top and thread with a ribbon for chocolate ornaments, then use a contrasting chocolate to decorate with design or names.

Chocolate Drizzles

You can have great fun making random shapes or, with a steady hand, special designs.

1 Melt chocolate and pour into a paper cone (see right) or small icing bag fitted with a very small plain nozzle (tip). Drizzle on to a waxed paper-lined cookie sheet in small, self-contained lattice shapes, such as circles or squares, allow to set until firm (about 30 minutes) before carefully peeling off paper.

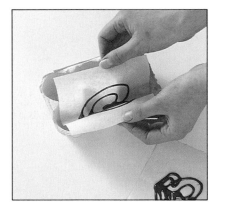

2 Chocolate can be used in many designs such as flowers or butterflies. Use waxed paper as tracing paper and pipe chocolate over the chosen design or shape as a guide.

3 For butterflies, pipe chocolate on to individually cut squares and leave until just beginning to set. Use a long, thin box (such as an egg carton) and place the butterfly shape in the box or between the cups so it is bent in the center, creating the butterfly shape. Chill until needed.

Chocolate Leaves

You can use any fresh, non-toxic leaf with distinct veins such as rose, bay or lemon leaves.

1 Wash and dry leaves thoroughly. Melt the chocolate and use a pastry brush or spoon to coat the veined side of leaf completely.

2 Place the coated leaves chocolate-side up on a waxed paper-lined cookie sheet to set.

3 Starting at the stem end, gently peel away the leaf and store chocolate leaves in a cool place until needed.

Making a Paper Cone

A paper cone is ideal for piping small amounts of messy liquids like chocolate as it is small, easy to handle and disposable, avoiding the cleaning of an icing bag.

Chocolate Cups

Large or small cup-liners or candy cases can be used to make cases to fill with ice creams, mousses or liqueurs. Use double liners inside each other for extra support.

1 Fold a square of waxed paper in half to form a triangle. With the triangle point facing you, fold the left corner down to the center.

2 Fold the right corner down and wrap completely around folded left corner, forming a cone. Fold the ends into the cone. Spoon the melted chocolate or liquid into cone and fold top edges over to enclose the filling.

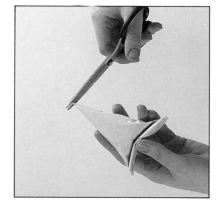

3 When ready to pipe, snip off the end of the point to make a hole about ⅛ in in diameter. Use to pipe chocolates, white icings and melted preserves.

4 Another method is to use a small heavy-duty freezer or plastic bag. Fill as above, squeezing the filling into one corner and twisting the top to seal. Snip off the corner of the bag and squeeze gently to pipe.

1 Melt the chocolate and, using a spoon or pastry brush, completely coat the bottom and side of the case. Allow to set, then repeat for a second layer. Allow to set for several hours or overnight.

2 Carefully peel off the cup-liner or candy case, set on a cookie sheet and fill as desired.

Chocolate Layer Cake

The cake layers can be made ahead, wrapped and frozen for future use. Always defrost cakes completely before icing.

Serves 10–12

INGREDIENTS
unsweetened cocoa for dusting
8 oz can cooked whole
   beets, drained and juice
   reserved
½ cup unsalted butter,
   softened
2½ cups (packed) light brown sugar
3 eggs
1 tbsp vanilla extract
3 oz unsweetened chocolate, melted
2 cups flour
2 tsp baking powder
½ tsp salt
½ cup buttermilk
chocolate curls (optional)

CHOCOLATE GANACHE FROSTING
2 cups whipping or heavy
   cream
1 lb 2 oz fine quality, bittersweet or
   semi-sweet chocolate, chopped
1 tbsp vanilla extract

bittersweet chocolate

unsweetened chocolate

eggs

vanilla extract

beets

1 Preheat oven to 350°F. Grease two 9 in cake pans and dust bottom and sides with cocoa. Grate beets and add to beet juice. With electric mixer, beat the butter, brown sugar, eggs and vanilla extract until pale and fluffy, 3–5 minutes. Reduce speed and beat in chocolate.

2 In a bowl, sift flour, baking powder and salt. With mixer on low speed and beginning and ending with flour mixture, alternately beat in flour mixture in fourths and buttermilk in thirds. Add beets and juice and beat for 1 minute. Divide between pans and bake for 30–35 minutes. Remove to rack for 10 minutes or until a cake tester inserted in the centre comes out clean, then unmold.

3 To make the frosting, in a heavy-based saucepan over medium heat, heat cream until it just begins to boil, stirring occasionally to prevent it scorching. Remove from heat and stir in chocolate, stirring constantly until melted and smooth. Stir in vanilla. Strain into a bowl and refrigerate, stirring every 10 minutes, until spreadable, about 1 hour.

4 Assemble the cake. Place one layer on a serving plate and spread with one-third of the ganache. Turn cake layer bottom side up and spread remaining ganache over top and side of cake. If using, top with the chocolate curls. Allow ganache to set for 20–30 minutes, then refrigerate before serving.

Chocolate Mint-filled Cupcakes

For extra mint flavor, chop 8 thin mint cream-filled after dinner mints and fold into the cake batter before filling paper liners. Omit the cream filling if you wish.

Makes 12

INGREDIENTS
2 cups cake or pastry flour
1 tsp baking soda
pinch of salt
½ cup unsweetened cocoa
10 tbsp unsalted butter, softened
1½ cups superfine sugar
3 eggs
1 tsp peppermint extract
1 cup milk

MINT CREAM FILLING
1¼ cups heavy or whipping cream
1 tsp peppermint extract

CHOCOLATE MINT GLAZE
6 oz plain chocolate
½ cup unsalted butter
1 tsp peppermint extract

plain chocolate

eggs

cocoa

peppermint extract

1 Preheat oven to 350°F. Line 12 × 2½ in muffin cups with paper cases. Into a bowl, sift together flour, baking soda and cocoa. In a large mixing bowl with electric mixer, beat butter and sugar until light and creamy, about 3–5 minutes. Add eggs one at a time, beating well after each addition; beat in peppermint extract. On low speed, beat in flour-cocoa mixture alternately with milk, until just blended. Spoon into paper liners.

2 Bake for 12–15 minutes until cake tester inserted in center comes out clean, do not over-bake. Immediately remove cupcakes to wire rack to cool completely. When cool, remove paper cases. Prepare filling. In a small bowl with electric mixer, whip the cream and peppermint extract until stiff peaks form. Spoon into a small pastry bag fitted with a small plain tip. Push tip into the bottom of a cupcake and squeeze gently releasing about 1 tbsp of cream into center. Repeat with remaining cupcakes.

3 Prepare glaze. In a saucepan over low heat, melt chocolate and butter, stirring until smooth. Remove from heat and stir in peppermint extract. Cool, then spread on top of each cake.

Chocolate Chestnut Roulade

For an alternative decoration, dip 12 candied chestnuts halfway into melted plain chocolate, allow to set and use to decorate the roulade.

Serves 10–12

INGREDIENTS
6 oz bittersweet chocolate, chopped
2 tbsp cocoa, sifted
¼ cup strong coffee or espresso
6 eggs, separated
pinch of cream of tartar
6 tbsp superfine sugar
1 tsp vanilla extract
unsweetened cocoa for dusting
candied chestnuts to decorate

CHESTNUT CREAM FILLING
2 cups heavy cream
2 tbsp rum or coffee-flavor liqueur
1½ cups canned sweetened chestnut purée
4 oz bittersweet chocolate, grated

chestnut purée

bittersweet chocolate

cocoa

coffee-flavor liqueur

candied chestnuts

1 Preheat oven to 350°F. Grease bottom and sides of 15½ × 10½ × 1 in jelly roll pan. Line bottom with parchment paper, allowing 1 in overhang. In the top of a double boiler, over low heat, melt the chocolate, stirring frequently until smooth. Set aside. Dissolve the cocoa with the coffee to make a smooth paste. Set aside.

2 In a mixing bowl with electric mixer, beat egg yolks with half the sugar until pale and thick, about 3–5 minutes. Slowly beat in the melted chocolate and cocoa-coffee paste until just blended.

In a bowl with electric mixer, beat egg whites and cream of tartar until stiff peaks form. Sprinkle sugar over whites in two batches and beat until whites are stiff and glossy; beat in vanilla. Stir a spoonful of whites into chocolate mixture to lighten it, then fold in remaining whites. Spoon into pan. Bake for 20–25 minutes or until cake springs back when touched with a fingertip.

COOK'S TIP

Beating egg whites should always be the last step in preparation of cakes or any other recipes. Once they are beaten, they should be folded in immediately and never held.

3 Meanwhile, dust a dish towel with cocoa. When cake is done, turn out on to towel immediately and remove paper. Starting at a narrow end, roll cake and towel together jelly roll fashion. Cool completely.

4 Prepare filling. In a medium bowl with electric mixer, whip the cream and rum or liqueur until soft peaks form. Beat a spoonful of cream into the chestnut purée to lighten it, then fold in the remaining cream and grated chocolate. Reserve a quarter of chestnut cream mixture for garnish.

5 Assemble the roulade. Unroll roulade and, if you like, trim edges. Spread chestnut cream mixture to within 1 in of edge of the cake. Using the towel to lift the cake, gently roll cake jelly roll fashion.

6 Place roulade seam-side down on a serving plate. Spread the reserved chestnut cream over the top of the roulade, and spoon some into small pastry bag fitted with a medium star tip. Pipe rosettes down the sides of roulade and decorate with candied chestnuts.

Marbled Chocolate-Peanut Butter Cake

This cake cannot be tested with a cake tester because the peanut butter remains soft in the center. Rely on the fingertip method: the cake should spring back when touched after 50–60 minutes.

Serves 12–14

INGREDIENTS
4 oz unsweetened chocolate, chopped
1 cup unsalted butter, softened
1 cup smooth or chunky peanut butter
1 cup granulated sugar
1 cup packed light brown sugar
5 eggs
2 cups flour
2 tsp baking powder
½ tsp salt
½ cup milk
⅓ cup chocolate chips

CHOCOLATE PEANUT BUTTER GLAZE
2 tbsp butter, cut up
2 tbsp smooth peanut butter
3 tbsp corn syrup
1 tsp vanilla extract
6 oz plain chocolate, broken into pieces

peanut butter

unsweetened chocolate

chocolate chips

brown sugar

1 Preheat oven to 350°F. Generously grease and flour a 12 cup tube or ring mold. In the top of a double boiler over low heat, melt the chocolate.

4 Pour half the batter into another bowl. Stir the melted chocolate into one half of the batter until well blended. Stir the chocolate chips into the other half of the batter.

2 In a large mixing bowl with electric mixer, beat butter, peanut butter and sugars until light and creamy, about 3–5 minutes, scraping side of bowl occasionally. Add eggs one at a time, beating well after each addition.

5 Using a large spoon, drop alternate spoonfuls of chocolate batter and peanut butter batter into the prepared pan. Using a knife, pull through the batters to create a swirled marbled effect; do not let the knife touch side or bottom of pan and do not over-mix. Bake the cake for 50–60 minutes until top of cake springs back when touched with a fingertip. Cool cake in the pan on wire rack for 10 minutes. Unmold on to rack to cool completely.

3 In a medium bowl, stir together flour, baking powder and salt. Add to the butter mixture alternately with the milk until just blended.

6 Prepare glaze. In a small saucepan combine all the ingredients and 1 tbsp water. Melt over low heat, stirring until well blended and smooth. Cool slightly. When slightly thickened, drizzle glaze over cake allowing it to run down side.

Chocolate Pecan Torte

This torte uses finely ground nuts instead of flour. Toast then cool the nuts before grinding finely in a food processor. Do not over grind the nuts, as the oils will form a paste.

Serves 16

INGREDIENTS

7 oz bittersweet or plain chocolate, chopped
10 tbsp unsalted butter, cut into pieces
4 eggs
½ cup superfine sugar
2 tsp vanilla extract
1 cup ground pecans
2 tsp ground cinnamon
24 toasted pecan halves to decorate (optional)

CHOCOLATE HONEY GLAZE

4 oz bittersweet or semi-sweet chocolate, chopped
¼ cup unsalted butter, cut into pieces
2 tbsp honey
pinch of ground cinnamon

plain chocolate

vanilla extract

eggs

honey

cinnamon

pecans

1 Preheat oven to 350°F. Grease an 8 × 2½ in springform pan; line bottom with waxed paper then grease the paper. Wrap bottom and side of pan with foil to prevent water seeping in. In a saucepan over a low heat, melt chocolate and butter, stirring until smooth. Remove from heat. In a mixing bowl with electric mixer, beat eggs, sugar and vanilla until frothy, 1–2 minutes. Stir in melted chocolate, ground nuts and cinnamon. Pour into pan.

2 Place foil-wrapped pan in a large roasting pan and pour boiling water into roasting pan, to come ¾ in up the side of the springform pan. Bake for 25–30 minutes until edge of cake is set, but center is soft. Remove from water bath and remove foil. Cool on rack.

3 Prepare glaze. In a small saucepan over low heat, melt chocolate, butter, honey and cinnamon, stirring until smooth; remove from heat. Carefully dip toasted pecan halves halfway into glaze and place on waxed paper-lined cookie sheet until set. The glaze will have thickened slightly.

4 Remove side from springform pan and invert cake on to wire rack. Remove the pan bottom and paper, so bottom of cake is now the top. Pour thickened glaze over cake, tilting rack slightly to spread glaze. Use a metal spatula to smooth sides. Arrange nuts around outside edge of torte and allow glaze to set.

French Chocolate Cake

This very dense chocolate cake can be made up to 3 days before serving, but decorate with icing sugar on the day it is to be served.

Serves 10

INGREDIENTS
9 oz bittersweet chocolate, chopped
1 cup unsalted butter, cut into pieces
½ cup granulated sugar
2 tbsp brandy or orange-flavor liqueur
5 eggs
1 tbsp plain flour
confectioners' sugar for dusting
whipped cream or sour cream for serving

bittersweet chocolate

eggs

brandy

1 Preheat oven to 350°F. Generously grease a 9 × 2 in springform pan. Line bottom with waxed paper and grease the paper. Wrap bottom and side of pan in foil to prevent water seeping into cake. In a saucepan over a low heat, melt chocolate, butter and sugar, stirring frequently until smooth; cool slightly. Stir in the liqueur. In a large mixing bowl with electric mixer, beat eggs lightly, about 1 minute. Beat in flour then slowly beat in the chocolate mixture until well blended. Pour into pan.

2 Place filled, foil-wrapped pan in a large roasting pan and pour boiling water into roasting pan, to come ¾ in up the side of the springform pan. Bake for 25–30 minutes until edge of cake is set, but center is still soft. Remove pan from water bath and remove foil. Cool on wire rack completely (cake will sink in the center and may crack).

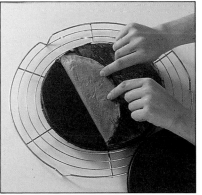

3 Remove side of springform pan and turn cake on to wire rack. Remove springform pan bottom and paper, so the bottom of cake is now the top.

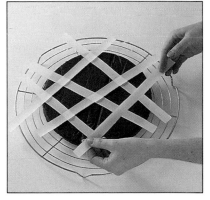

4 Cut 6–8 strips of waxed paper 1 in wide and place randomly over cake or make a lattice-style pattern if you wish. Dust cake with confectioners' sugar; then carefully remove paper. Slide cake on to a serving plate and serve with cream.

White Chocolate Mousse and Strawberry Layer Cake

The strawberries used in this cake can be replaced by raspberries or blackberries and the appropriate flavor liqueur.

Serves 10

INGREDIENTS

4 oz fine quality white chocolate, chopped
½ cup whipping or heavy cream
½ cup milk
1 tbsp rum or vanilla extract
8 tbsp unsalted butter, softened
¾ cup granulated sugar
3 eggs
2 cups flour
1 tsp baking powder
pinch of salt
1½ lb fresh strawberries, sliced, plus extra for decoration
3 cups whipping cream
2 tbsp rum or strawberry-flavor liqueur

WHITE CHOCOLATE MOUSSE FILLING

9 oz fine quality white chocolate, chopped
1½ cups whipping or heavy cream
2 tbsp rum or strawberry-flavor liqueur

strawberries

1 Preheat oven to 350°F. Grease and flour two 9 × 2 in cake pans. Line the base of the pans with baking parchment. Melt chocolate and cream in a double boiler over a low heat, stirring until smooth. Stir in milk and rum or vanilla extract; set aside to cool.

4 Prepare mousse. In medium saucepan over low heat, melt chocolate and cream until smooth, stirring frequently. Stir in rum or strawberry-flavor liqueur and pour into a bowl. Refrigerate until mixture is just set. With a wire whisk, whip lightly until mixture has a 'mousse' consistency.

white chocolate

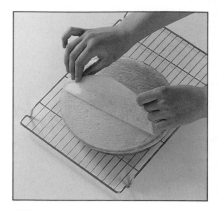

2 In a large mixing bowl with electric mixer, beat the butter and sugar until light and creamy, about 3–5 minutes, scraping sides of bowl occasionally. Add eggs one at a time, beating well after each addition. In a small bowl, stir together flour, baking powder and salt. Alternately add flour and melted chocolate to eggs in batches, just until blended. Pour batter into pans and spread evenly.

5 Assemble cake. With serrated knife, slice both cake layers in half crosswise, making four layers. Place one layer on plate and spread one third of mousse on top. Arrange about one third of sliced strawberries over mousse. Place second layer on top and spread with another third of mousse. Arrange another third of sliced strawberries over mousse. Place third layer on top and spread with remaining mousse and cover with remaining sliced strawberries. Cover with last cake layer.

3 Bake for 20–25 minutes until cake tester inserted in center comes out clean. Cool on wire rack for 10 minutes. Turn cakes out on to wire rack, peel off paper and cool completely.

6 Whip the cream with the rum or liqueur until firm peaks form. Spread about half the whipped cream over top and sides of cake. Spoon remaining cream into a decorating bag fitted with a medium star tip and pipe scrolls on top of cake. Garnish with remaining strawberries.

Luxury White Chocolate Cheesecake

To ensure an even crust, use a dessert spoon or tablespoon to press crumbs to bottom and side of pan.

Serves 16–20

INGREDIENTS
5 oz (about 16–18) wholewheat
    digestive cookies
½ cup blanched hazelnuts,
    toasted
4 tbsp unsalted butter, melted
½ tsp ground cinnamon

FILLING
12 oz fine quality white chocolate,
    chopped
½ cup whipping or heavy cream
3 × 8 oz packages cream cheese,
    softened
⅓ cup granulated sugar
4 eggs
2 tbsp hazelnut-flavor liqueur or
    1 tbsp vanilla extract

TOPPING
1¾ cup sour cream
¼ cup granulated sugar
1 tbsp hazelnut-flavor liqueur or
    1 tsp vanilla extract
white chocolate curls to decorate
cocoa for dusting (optional)

digestive cookies

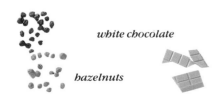

white chocolate

hazelnuts

1 Preheat oven to 350°F. Lightly grease a 9 × 3 in springform pan. In a food processor with metal blade, process cookies and hazelnuts until fine crumbs form. Pour in butter and cinnamon. Process just until blended. Using the back of a spoon, press on to bottom and to within ½ in of top of side of pan. Bake for 5–7 minutes, until just set. Remove to rack to cool. Lower oven temperature to 300°F.

2 Prepare filling. In a small saucepan over a low heat, melt the white chocolate and cream until smooth, stirring frequently. Set aside to cool.

4 Prepare topping. In a small bowl whisk the sour cream, sugar and liqueur or vanilla. Pour over cheesecake, spreading evenly, and return to oven. Bake for a further 5–7 minutes. Turn off oven, but do not open door and allow cake to stand for 1 hour.

3 In a large bowl with an electric mixer, beat the cream cheese and sugar until smooth, about 2–4 minutes. Add eggs one at a time, beating well after each addition, scraping bowl occasionally. Slowly beat in the white chocolate mixture and liqueur or vanilla extract.

Pour into baked crust. Place pan on cookie sheet. Bake for 45–55 minutes, or until edge of cake is firm but center is still slightly soft, do not allow to brown. Remove to wire rack while preparing topping. Increase oven temperature to 400°F.

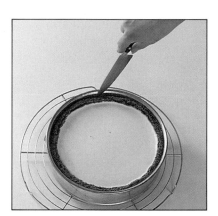

5 Remove to wire rack to cool to room temperature. Run sharp knife around edge of cake in pan to separate it from side; this helps prevent cracking. Cool completely then refrigerate, loosely covered, overnight.

6 To serve, run sharp knife around edge of pan to loosen cake. Remove side of springform pan. If you like, slide sharp knife under crust to separate cake from bottom and with metal spatula, slide on to serving plate. Alternatively, leave cake on pan bottom to avoid breaking crust or surface and serve from bottom of pan. Decorate top of cake with chocolate curls and dust lightly with cocoa.

Mississippi Mud Cake

There are many versions of this cake, but all of them are based on a dark cocoa-based chocolate cake, which is meant to be reminiscent of the cocoa-black shores of the Mississippi River.

Serves 8–10

INGREDIENTS
2 cups flour
1 tsp baking powder
5 oz unsweetened chocolate
1 cup unsalted butter
1¼ cups strong coffee or espresso
pinch of salt
2 cups granulated sugar
¼ cup bourbon or whisky
2 eggs, slightly beaten
2 tsp vanilla extract
1 cup sweetened shredded coconut
cocoa for dusting
1½ cups whipping or heavy cream
1 tsp vanilla extract
Coconut Ruffles (see step 6)

FILLING
1 cup evaporated milk
½ cup (packed) light or dark brown
  sugar
8 tbsp unsalted butter
3 oz plain chocolate
3 egg yolks, lightly beaten
1 tsp vanilla extract
2 cups pecans, chopped
1 cup miniature marshmallows

1 Preheat the oven to 350°F. Grease 2 × 9 in cake pans, dust bottoms and sides with cocoa. In a bowl sift flour and baking powder. In a saucepan over low heat, melt chocolate, butter, coffee, salt and sugar, stirring occasionally until smooth and sugar dissolved. Stir in bourbon or whisky. Pour chocolate mixture into a bowl and cool slightly. With an electric mixer on medium speed, beat in eggs and vanilla, decrease speed and beat in the flour; stir in coconut. Pour into prepared pans.

2 Bake for 25–30 minutes until cake tester inserted in center comes out with just a few crumbs attached; do not over-bake or the cake will be too dry. Cool on wire rack for 10 minutes. Remove cakes from the pans and place on a wire rack to cool completely.

3 In a large heavy-based saucepan, combine the evaporated milk, sugar, butter, chocolate, egg yolks and vanilla. Cook over medium heat, stirring frequently for 8–10 minutes until chocolate is melted and smooth and mixture is thick enough to coat the back of a wooden spoon; do not boil or mixture will curdle. Remove from heat and stir in nuts and marshmallows, stirring until melted. Refrigerate until thick enough to spread, stirring occasionally to prevent a skin forming.

pecans

plain chocolate

miniature marshmallows

unsweetened chocolate

shredded coconut

eggs

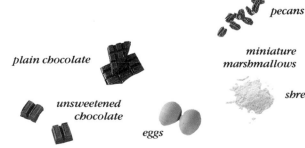

4 Assemble cake. With serrated knife, slice both cake layers in half crosswise, making four layers. Spread each of the bottom cake layers with half the chocolate nut filling and cover each bottom half with its respective top layer.

5 In a medium bowl, whip the cream and the vanilla until firm peaks form. Place one filled cake layer on a cake plate and spread with half the whipped cream. Top with the second filled cake layer and spread with the remaining cream, swirling cream to form an attractive pattern.

6 Make the Coconut Ruffles. Using a heavy hammer and nail, puncture the eyes of a fresh coconut. Drain off the liquid and reserve if wished. Place coconut in a strong plastic bag and hit shell very hard with the hammer to crack coconut open. With a strong blunt-bladed knife, separate the flesh from the shell; it will break into medium sized pieces. Rinse pieces under cold running water and store in cold water. With a swivel-bladed vegetable peeler, draw the blade along the curved edge of a coconut piece to make thin wide curls with a brown edge.

Chocolate Cappuccino Cake

If desired the cake can be left whole and rolled roulade-style, or baked in 2 × 9 in pans for a round cake.

Serves 8–10

INGREDIENTS
6 oz plain chocolate, chopped
2 tsp instant espresso powder (or
   1 tbsp instant coffee powder)
   dissolved in 3 tbsp boiling water
6 eggs, separated
¾ cup granulated sugar
pinch of cream of tartar
unsweetened cocoa for sifting
chocolate coffee beans to decorate

COFFEE CREAM FILLING
¾ cup whipping or heavy cream
2 tbsp granulated sugar
8 oz mascarpone or cream cheese,
   softened
2 tbsp coffee-flavor liqueur
1 oz plain chocolate, grated

COFFEE BUTTERCREAM
4 egg yolks, at room temperature
⅓ cup corn syrup
⅓ cup granulated sugar
1 cup unsalted butter, cut into small
   pieces and softened
1 tbsp instant espresso powder
   dissolved in 1–2 tsp boiling water
1–2 tbsp coffee-flavor liqueur

1 Preheat oven to 350°F. Grease a 15½ × 10½ in cookie sheet. Line with non-stick baking parchment or waxed paper, leaving a 2 in overhang on each narrow end. Grease the paper. In the top of a double boiler, over low heat, heat chocolate and dissolved coffee powder until melted and smooth, stirring frequently. Set aside. In a bowl with an electric mixer, beat yolks and sugar until thick and light-colored, 3–5 minutes. Reduce speed to low and beat in chocolate mixture until blended.

2 In a large bowl with electric mixer with cleaned beaters, beat the egg whites and cream of tartar until stiff peaks begin to form. Do not overbeat. Stir a spoonful of whites into the chocolate mixture to lighten it, then fold in remaining whites. Pour batter into the prepared pan, spreading into corners and smoothing the top evenly. Bake for 12–15 minutes until top springs back when touched lightly with a fingertip. Sprinkle clean dish towel with cocoa to cover and turn cake out on to towel. Peel off paper and cool.

3 Prepare filling. In a medium bowl with an electric mixer, whip the cream and sugar until soft peaks form. In another bowl, beat the mascarpone or cream cheese and liqueur until light and smooth. Stir in the grated chocolate and fold in the whipped cream. Cover and refrigerate until ready for use.

4 Prepare buttercream. In a bowl with an electric mixer on high speed, beat yolks until thick and pale-colored, 5–6 minutes. In a saucepan over medium heat, cook syrup and sugar until mixture boils, stirring constantly. With mixer on medium-low speed, slowly pour hot syrup over beaten yolks in a slow stream. Continue beating until mixture feels cool, 5–6 minutes. Beat in butter a few pieces at a time until mixture is smooth. Beat in diluted coffee and liqueur. Refrigerate until ready to use, but bring to room temperature before spreading.

cocoa

instant coffee powder

plain chocolate

eggs

chocolate coffee beans

5 Assemble cake. With a serrated knife, trim off any crisp edges of cake. Cut cake crosswise into three equal strips. Place one cake strip on a cake plate and spread with half the coffee cream filling. Cover with a second cake strip and the remaining filling. Top with the remaining cake strip.

6 Spoon about one third coffee buttercream into a small decorating bag fitted with a small star tip. Spread remaining buttercream on top and sides of cake. Pipe lattice or scroll design on top of cake and around edges of cake and decorate with chocolate coffee beans. Refrigerate cake if not serving immediately, but allow to stand at room temperature 30 minutes before serving.

Chocolate Pine Nut Tart

Lemon zest could be used instead of orange and a combination of white and plain chocolates substituted for all plain.

Serves 8

INGREDIENTS
1½ cups flour
¼ cup superfine sugar
pinch of salt
grated zest of ½ orange
½ cup unsalted butter, cut into small
　pieces
3 egg yolks, lightly beaten
1–2 tbsp iced water

FILLING
2 eggs
3 tbsp superfine sugar
grated zest of 1 orange
1 tbsp orange-flavor liqueur
1 cup whipping cream
4 oz plain chocolate, chopped
¾ cup pine nuts, toasted

TO DECORATE
1 orange
¼ cup granulated sugar
½ cup water

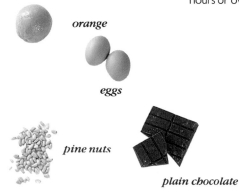

orange

eggs

pine nuts

plain chocolate

1 In a food processor with metal blade, process flour, sugar, salt and zest to blend Add butter and process for 20–30 seconds until mixture resembles coarse crumbs. Add yolks and using pulse-action process until dough begins to stick together; do not allow dough to form a ball or pastry will be tough. If dough appears dry, add 1–2 tbsp iced water, little by little, just until dough holds together. Turn dough on to lightly floured surface and knead gently until blended. Shape into flat disc and wrap in waxed paper or clear plastic. Refrigerate for 2–3 hours or overnight.

2 Lightly butter a 9 in tart pan with removable bottom. Soften dough for 5–10 minutes at room temperature. On a well-floured surface, roll out dough into an 11 in round, about ⅛ in thick. Roll dough loosely around rolling pin and unroll over tart pan. Ease dough into pan. With floured fingers, press overhang down slightly towards center (making top edge thicker).

3 Roll a rolling pin over edge to cut off excess dough. Now press thicker top edge against side of pan to form rim slightly higher than pan. Prick bottom with fork. Refrigerate for 1 hour. Preheat oven to 400°F. Line tart pan with foil or waxed paper; fill with dry beans or rice. Bake for 5 minutes, then lift out foil with beans and bake 5 more minutes, until set. Remove to wire rack to cool slightly. Lower temperature to 350°F.

4 Prepare filling. In a medium bowl beat the eggs, sugar, zest and liqueur. Blend in the cream. Sprinkle the chocolate evenly over bottom of tart shell, then sprinkle over pine nuts. Place pan on cookie sheet and gently pour egg and cream mixture into tart shell. Bake tart for 20–30 minutes, until pastry is golden and custard is set. Remove to wire rack to cool slightly.

5 Prepare decoration. With vegetable peeler, remove thin strips of orange zest and cut into julienne strips. In a small saucepan over high heat, bring julienne strips, sugar and water to a boil. Boil for 5–8 minutes until syrup is thickened; then stir in 1 tbsp cold water to stop cooking.

6 With a pastry brush, carefully glaze tart with the orange-sugar syrup and arrange julienne orange strips over tart. Remove side of tart pan and slide tart on to plate. Serve warm.

COOK'S TIP
If you do not wish to prepare the garnish, simply heat 2 tbsp marmalade and 1 tsp water until dissolved. Brush over surface of warm tart.

Chocolate Chip Pecan Pie

Bittersweet chocolate can be substituted for unsweetened chocolate, but use only ½ cup brown sugar and ½ cup corn syrup or the tart will be too sweet.

Serves 8–10

INGREDIENTS
1¼ cups flour
1 tbsp superfine sugar
½ tsp salt
½ cup unsalted butter, cut into small pieces
½ cup iced water

FILLING
3 oz unsweetened chocolate, chopped
4 tbsp butter, cut into pieces
3 eggs
¾ cup packed light or dark brown sugar
¾ cup corn syrup
1 tbsp vanilla extract
½ cup plain chocolate chips
2 cups pecan halves

unsweetened chocolate

eggs

vanilla extract

chocolate chips

pecans

1 Prepare pastry. In a food processor fitted with a metal blade, process flour, sugar and salt to blend. Add butter and process for 15–20 seconds until mixture resembles coarse crumbs. With machine running, add iced water through feed tube, just until dough begins to stick together; do not allow dough to form a ball or pastry will be tough. Turn dough on to floured work surface, shape into flat disc and wrap tightly in waxed paper or plastic wrap. Refrigerate for 1 hour.

Lightly butter a 9 in pie pan. Soften dough for 10–15 minutes at room temperature. On a well-floured surface, roll out dough into a 12 in round, about ⅛ in thick. Roll dough loosely around rolling pin and unroll over pie pan. Ease dough into pan.

2 With kitchen scissors, trim the pastry even with the rim of the pie pan; using fingers, flatten to rim of pie pan. Re-roll trimmings to a long rectangle and, with a sharp knife, cut thin strips about ¼ in wide. Braid three strips together. Repeat until you have sufficient braids to fit around the pie edge. Brush pastry edge with water and press pastry braids to edge. Prick bottom of dough with fork. Refrigerate for 30 minutes.

3 Preheat oven to 400°F. Line pie shell with foil or waxed paper; fill with dry beans or rice. Bake for 5 minutes, carefully lift out foil with beans and bake for 5 more minutes. Remove to wire rack to cool slightly. Lower oven temperature to 375°F.

4 Prepare filling. In a small saucepan over low heat, melt the chocolate and butter, stirring until smooth. Set aside to cool slightly.

COOK'S TIP

This pie can also be made in a tart pan with a removable bottom. Try to arrange the pecans in concentric circles for a more sophisticated looking tart.

5 In a medium bowl, beat the eggs with the sugar, syrup and vanilla. Slowly beat in the melted chocolate.

6 Arrange pecan halves and chocolate chips over bottom of pastry. Place pie pan on cookie sheet and carefully pour chocolate-sugar mixture into shell. Bake 35–45 minutes, until chocolate mixture is set (top may crack slightly). If pastry edge begins to brown too quickly, cover with strips of foil. Remove to wire rack to cool. Serve warm or chilled, with softly whipped cream.

Chocolate Banana Toffee Pie

The crust can be baked ahead and filled with the toffee and chocolate layers, then refrigerated. Do not add the bananas and cream until a few hours before serving.

Serves 12–14

INGREDIENTS
2 × 14 fl oz cans sweetened
 condensed milk
5 oz bittersweet chocolate, broken in
 pieces
⅔ cup whipping or heavy cream
2 tsp corn syrup
3 tbsp unsalted butter, cut into pieces
1 tsp vanilla extract

GINGER CRUMB CRUST
about 24–26 ginger snaps, crushed
6 tbsp butter, melted

TOPPING
5 oz fine quality white chocolate
2 cups heavy cream
3 ripe bananas
white chocolate curls (optional)
unsweetened cocoa for dusting

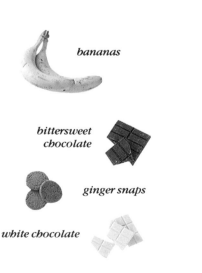

bananas

bittersweet chocolate

ginger snaps

white chocolate

1 To make 'toffee', puncture a small hole in each can of milk to release pressure. Place them in a saucepan large enough to cover with water. Bring water to a boil over medium heat. Reduce heat and simmer 2 hours, partially covered; top up with water if necessary. Remove cans from water and cool.

Prepare the crust. Preheat oven to 350°F. Grease a 9 in loose bottomed tart pan, 1½ in deep. Mix ginger crumbs with butter and pat on to bottom and side of pan. Bake for 5–7 minutes until set.

2 In a medium saucepan combine the chocolate, cream and corn syrup. Over medium heat, bring to a simmer, stirring frequently until melted and smooth. Remove from heat and beat in butter and vanilla. Pour into cooled crust and refrigerate until set, about 1 hour.

3 Open cans of cooked milk and empty into a bowl. With a wire whisk beat until smooth. Spoon over the chocolate layer. In a food processor with metal disc, process chocolate into small crumbs. In a small saucepan, over medium heat, heat ½ cup of the cream until bubbles form around the edge.

With machine running, pour in cream and process until chocolate is melted. Strain into a bowl and refrigerate for 25–30 minutes, until cold but not too thick. With an electric mixer, whip remaining cream until stiff. Beat in a spoonful of cream to the chocolate mixture, then fold in remaining cream.

4 Thinly slice the bananas and arrange over toffee layer in tart pan. Spoon over the chocolate whipped cream, spreading to the edge. Decorate with chocolate curls and a light dusting of cocoa.

Truffle-filled Filo Tulips

The cups can be prepared a day ahead and stored in an airtight container.

Makes about 24 cups

INGREDIENTS
3–6 sheets fresh or frozen (thawed)
   filo pastry, depending on size
3 tbsp unsalted butter, melted
sugar for sprinkling
lemon zest to decorate (optional)

CHOCOLATE TRUFFLE MIXTURE
1 cup heavy cream
8 oz bittersweet or semi-sweet
   chocolate, chopped
4 tbsp unsalted butter, cut into pieces
2 tbsp brandy or other liqueur

filo pastry

lemon

brandy

bittersweet chocolate

1 Prepare truffle mixture. In a saucepan over medium heat, bring cream to a boil. Remove from heat and add chocolate, stirring until melted. Beat in butter and add brandy. Strain into a bowl. Refrigerate for 1 hour until thick.

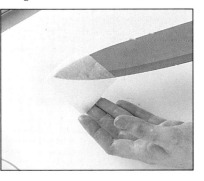

2 Preheat oven to 400°F. Grease a muffin pan with 24 × 1½ in cups. Place filo sheets on a work surface. Cut each sheet into 2½ in squares. Cover with damp dish towel. Keeping filo sheets covered, place one square on a work surface. Brush lightly with melted butter, turn over and brush other side. Sprinkle with a pinch of sugar. Butter another square and place it over the first at an angle; sprinkle with sugar. Butter a third square and place over the first two, unevenly, so corners form an uneven edge. Press the layered square into the pan. Continue to fill the pan.

3 Bake the filo cups for 4–6 minutes, until golden. Cool for 10 minutes in the pan on a wire rack. Remove from pan and cool completely.

4 Stir the chocolate mixture; it should be just thick enough to pipe. Spoon mixture into a piping bag with a medium star tip and pipe a swirl into each cup. Decorate each with a lemon curl.

Chocolate Lemon Tartlets

Pastry tartlets can be prepared a day ahead but are best filled just a few hours before serving so the fillings are still soft. An easy way to bake tartlet shells is to use muffin or cupcake liners. One small liner just covers the bottom and side of a 3 in tartlet.

Makes 12 tartlets

INGREDIENTS
Follow the pastry recipe on page 36, substituting lemon zest for the orange zest.
grated zest of lemon
lemon twists to decorate

LEMON CUSTARD SAUCE
zest and juice of 1 lemon
1½ cups milk
6 egg yolks
⅓ cup superfine sugar

LEMON CURD FILLING
grated zest and juice of 2 lemons
¾ cup unsalted butter, cut into pieces
2 cups granulated sugar
3 eggs, lightly beaten

CHOCOLATE LAYER
¾ cup heavy cream
6 oz bittersweet or semi-sweet chocolate, chopped
2 tbsp unsalted butter, cut into pieces

lemon

eggs

bittersweet chocolate

1 Prepare custard sauce. Place zest in a saucepan with the milk and over medium heat, bring to a boil. Remove from heat and stand for 5 minutes to infuse. Reheat milk gently. In a bowl with an electric mixer, beat yolks and sugar until pale and thick, 2–3 minutes. Pour over about 1 cup hot milk, beating vigorously. Return yolk mixture to the pan and cook gently, stirring constantly, over low heat, until the mixture thickens and lightly coats back of a spoon. (Do not allow sauce to boil or it will curdle.) Strain into a chilled bowl. Stir 2 tbsp lemon juice into sauce. Cool, stirring occasionally, then refrigerate until ready to use.

2 Prepare pastry as on page 36. Prepare lemon curd filling. Combine the lemon zest, juice, butter and sugar in the top of a double boiler. Over medium heat, heat until butter is melted and sugar dissolved. Reduce heat to low. Stir lightly beaten eggs into butter mixture. Cook over low heat, stirring constantly, until mixture thickens and coats the back of a spoon (about 15 minutes). Pour (or strain if you do not want the lemon zest) into a bowl. Cool, stirring occasionally. Refrigerate to thicken, stirring occasionally.

3 Lightly butter 12 × 3 in tartlet molds (if possible with removable bases). On a lightly floured surface, roll out pastry to ⅛ in thick. Using a 4 in fluted-edged cutter, cut out 12 rounds and press each one into tartlet molds. Prick base. Place molds on a cookie sheet and refrigerate for 30 minutes. Preheat oven to 375°F. Cut out rounds of foil and line each mold; fill with dry beans or rice. Bake for 5–8 minutes. Remove foil with beans and bake for 5 more minutes, until golden. Remove to rack to cool.

4 Prepare chocolate layer. In a saucepan over medium heat, bring cream to a boil. Remove from heat and add chocolate all at once; stir until melted. Beat in butter and cool slightly. Pour filling into each tartlet mold to make a layer ¼ in thick. Refrigerate for 10 minutes until set. Remove tartlets from molds and spoon in a layer of lemon curd to come to the top of the pastry. Set aside, but do not refrigerate or chocolate layer will be too firm.

To serve, spoon a little custard on to a plate and place a tartlet in the center. Decorate with a lemon twist or drop rounds of chocolate in the custard. Draw a skewer through chocolate to make 'heart' motifs.

Rich Chocolate-Berry Tart with Blackberry Sauce

Raspberries, blackberries, wild strawberries, boysenberries or loganberries, or any combination, can be used to top this tart. Likewise, the sauce can be made with the same berry or from a berry with a complementary flavor.

Serves 10

INGREDIENTS
½ cup unsalted butter, softened
½ cup superfine sugar
½ tsp salt
1 tbsp vanilla extract
½ cup unsweetened cocoa
   (preferably Dutch-processed)
1½ cups flour
1 lb fresh berries for topping

CHOCOLATE GANACHE FILLING
2 cups heavy cream
½ cup seedless blackberry or
   raspberry preserve
8 oz bittersweet chocolate, chopped
2 tbsp unsalted butter, cut into pieces

BLACKBERRY SAUCE
8 oz fresh or frozen blackberries or
   raspberries
1 tbsp lemon juice
2 tbsp superfine sugar
2 tbsp blackberry or raspberry-flavor
   liqueur

berries

chocolate

1 Prepare pastry. In a food processor fitted with metal blade, process butter, sugar, salt and vanilla until creamy. Add cocoa and process for 1 minute, until well blended; scrape side of bowl. Add flour all at once and using the pulse action, process for 10–15 seconds, until just blended. Place a piece of plastic wrap on work surface. Remove metal blade and turn out dough on to plastic wrap. Use wrap to help shape dough into flat disc and wrap tightly. Refrigerate for 1 hour.

2 Lightly grease a 9 in tart pan with removable base. Soften dough for 5–10 minutes at room temperature. Roll out dough between two sheets of waxed paper or plastic wrap to a 11 in round, about ¼ in thick. Peel off top sheet of plastic and invert dough into prepared pan. Ease dough into pan. Remove plastic wrap.

3 With floured fingers, press dough on to base and side of pan, then roll rolling pin over edge of pan to cut off any excess dough. Prick base of dough with fork. Refrigerate for 1 hour. Preheat oven to 350°F. Line tart shell with foil or parchment paper; fill with dry beans or rice. Bake for 10 minutes; lift out foil with beans and bake for 5 minutes more, until just set (pastry may look underdone on the bottom, but will dry out). Remove to wire rack to cool completely.

4 Prepare filling. In a medium saucepan over medium heat, bring cream and blackberry preserve to a boil. Remove from heat and add chocolate all at once, stirring until melted and smooth. Stir in butter and strain into cooled tart shell, smoothing top. Cool tart completely.

5 Prepare sauce. In a food processor combine blackberries, lemon juice and sugar and process until smooth. Strain into a small bowl and add blackberry-flavor liqueur. If sauce is too thick, thin with a little water.

6 To serve, remove tart from pan. Place on serving plate and arrange the blackberries on the top of the tart. With a pastry brush, brush berries with a little of the blackberry sauce to glaze lightly. Serve remaining sauce separately.

COOK'S TIP

This chocolate pastry has a cookie-like texture and is difficult to handle. If it is too soft to roll, place the dough into the pan and use lightly floured fingers to press the dough into the bottom and up the side of the pan.

Chocolate Cream Puffs

When making choux pastry, the butter should be completely melted just as the water comes to the boil. Do not allow the water to continue to boil or the proportion of water to flour will not remain accurate.

Makes 12 large or 24 small cream puffs

INGREDIENTS
1 cup flour
2 tbsp unsweetened cocoa
1 cup water
½ tsp salt
1 tbsp granulated sugar
½ cup unsalted butter, cut into pieces
4–5 eggs

CHOCOLATE PASTRY CREAM
5 oz plain chocolate, chopped
2 cups milk
6 egg yolks
½ cup granulated sugar
⅓ cup flour
½ cup whipping cream

CHOCOLATE GLAZE
1¼ cups whipping cream
4 tbsp unsalted butter, cut into pieces
8 oz bittersweet or semi-sweet chocolate, chopped
1 tbsp corn syrup
1 tsp vanilla extract

1 Preheat oven to 425°F. Lightly grease 1 or 2 large cookie sheets. Into a bowl sift together flour and cocoa. In a saucepan over medium heat, bring to a boil water, salt, sugar and butter (butter should just be melted when water boils). Remove from the heat and add flour mixture all at once, stirring vigorously until flour mixture is well blended and smooth and the mixture pulls away from the side of the pan. Return pan to the heat to cook pastry for 1 minute, beating constantly. Remove from heat.

bittersweet chocolate

eggs

cocoa

2 With an electric mixer (or by hand) beat in four of the eggs, one at a time, beating well after each addition, until each egg is well blended. Mixture should be thick and shiny and just fall from a spoon. If mixture is too dry, beat the fifth egg lightly and add to dough a little at a time until you reach a dropping consistency. Spoon mixture into a large piping bag fitted with a large star or plain tip. Pipe 12 mounds about 3 in across (or 24 small mounds) at least 2 in apart on the cookie sheet.

3 Bake for 35–40 minutes until puffed and firm. Remove puffs and turn off oven. Using a serrated knife, slice off top third of puff; return opened puffs, cut-side up, to cookie sheet and return to oven for 5–10 minutes to dry out. Remove to wire rack to cool completely.

4 Prepare pastry cream. Melt chocolate and set aside. Over medium heat, bring milk to a boil. In a bowl beat yolks and sugar until pale and thick, 3–5 minutes. Stir in flour. Slowly pour over about 1 cup hot milk into yolks, stirring constantly. Return yolk mixture to the saucepan and cook over medium heat until sauce boils. Cook for 1 minute; remove from heat and quickly stir in melted chocolate until blended.

Strain into a bowl and place a piece of plastic wrap against surface of custard (this prevents a skin forming). Cool to room temperature. Carefully peel plastic wrap from pastry cream. In a bowl with electric mixer, whip cream until firm peaks form. Fold into pastry cream.

5 Spoon pastry cream into a large piping bag fitted with a large star or plain tip. Fill each puff bottom with pastry cream, then cover each puff with its top. Arrange cream puffs on a large serving plate in a single layer or pile them up on top of each other.

6 To serve, in a medium saucepan over low heat, heat the cream, butter, chocolate, syrup and vanilla until melted and smooth, stirring frequently. Remove from heat and cool for 20–30 minutes until slightly thickened. Pour a little sauce over each of the cream puffs and serve while chocolate sauce is warm or refrigerate until ready to serve.

Chocolate Apricot Linzer Tart

To dust the top pastry strips only, cut ½ in wide strips of waxed paper at least 11 in long and place them between the pastry strips before dusting with confectioners' sugar.

Serves 10–12

INGREDIENTS
½ cup whole blanched almonds
⅔ cup superfine sugar
1½ cups flour
2 tbsp unsweetened cocoa
    (preferably Dutch-processed)
1 tsp ground cinnamon
½ tsp salt
1 tsp grated orange zest
1 cup unsalted butter, cut into pieces
2–3 tbsp iced water
½ cup plain mini-chocolate chips
confectioners' sugar for dusting

APRICOT FILLING
12 oz ready-to-eat dried apricots
½ cup orange juice
¾ cup water
3 tbsp granulated sugar
2 tbsp apricot preserve
½ tsp ground cinnamon
½ tsp almond extract

orange

apricots

cocoa

almonds

chocolate chips

1 Prepare filling. In a large saucepan over medium heat, bring the apricots, orange juice and water to a boil. Lower the heat and simmer gently for 15–20 minutes until apricots are very soft and the liquid is absorbed, stirring frequently to prevent sticking. Stir in sugar, apricot preserve, cinnamon and almond extract. Press mixture through a strainer into a bowl (or process in a food processor), cool then cover and refrigerate.

2 Prepare pastry. Lightly butter a 11 in tart pan with removable base. In a food processor with metal blade, process almonds with half the sugar until finely ground. Into a bowl, sift flour, cocoa, remaining sugar, cinnamon and salt. Add to food processor and process to blend. Add zest and butter and process for 15–20

seconds until mixture resembles coarse crumbs. Add 2 tbsp iced water and using pulse action, process until dough just begins to stick together; do not allow dough to form into a ball or pastry will be tough. If dough appears too dry add 1–2 tbsp more iced water, little by little, until dough holds together.

3 Turn dough on to lightly-floured work surface and knead lightly until just blended. Divide dough in half. With floured fingers, press half the dough on to bottom and side of pan. Prick base of dough with fork. Refrigerate for 30 minutes. Roll out remaining half of dough between 2 sheets of waxed paper or plastic wrap to a 11 in round; slide on to a cookie sheet and refrigerate for 30 minutes.

4 Preheat oven to 350°F. Spread filling on to base of pastry-lined pan. Sprinkle with chocolate chips. Set aside. Slide dough round on to lightly floured surface and cut into ½ in strips; allow the dough to soften for 3–5 minutes.

Place half the dough strips about ½ in apart over filling. Place remaining pastry strips diagonally across bottom strips about ½ in apart. With a fingertip, press down on each side of each crossing to accentuate lattice effect. Press ends to side of tart cutting off any excess.

Bake for 35–40 minutes until top of pastry is set and filling bubbles. Cool on rack to room temperature. To serve, remove side of pan, dust sugar over top pastry strips. Slide on to serving plate.

COOK'S TIP

Other dried fruits such as figs, prunes and pears go very well with chocolate. Any of these can be made into a paste as above and used as an alternative filling. For an easy filling, apricot or raspberry jam can be used. If you like, use dark, milk or white chocolate chips for contrast.

White Chocolate and Mango Cream Tart

To prevent a skin forming on the custard without stirring, dot the top with tiny cubes of butter. When ready to use, simply stir the butter into the custard.

Serves 8

INGREDIENTS
1 ½ cups flour
1 cup sweetened, shredded coconut
½ cup butter, softened
2 tbsp superfine sugar
2 egg yolks
½ tsp almond extract
2 ½ cups whipping cream
½ tsp almond extract
⅔ cup slivered almonds, toasted, to decorate

WHITE CHOCOLATE CUSTARD
5 oz fine quality white chocolate, chopped
½ cup whipping or heavy cream
⅓ cup cornstarch
1 tbsp flour
⅓ cup granulated sugar
1 ½ cups milk
5 egg yolks
1 large ripe mango

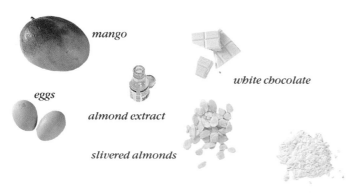

mango

eggs

almond extract

white chocolate

slivered almonds

shredded coconut

1 In a deep medium mixing bowl, with electric mixer at low speed, combine the flour, coconut, butter, sugar, egg yolks and almond extract until well blended. With fingers or back of a spoon, press pastry on to bottom and side of a lightly buttered 9 in tart pan, 1 ½ in deep with removable bottom. Prick base of dough with fork. Refrigerate for 30 minutes.

2 Preheat oven to 350°F. Line tart pan with foil or waxed paper; fill with dry beans or rice. Bake for 10 minutes. Lift out foil with beans and bake for 5–7 minutes more until golden. Remove to rack to cool completely.

3 Prepare filling. In a small saucepan over low heat, melt white chocolate with the cream, stirring until smooth. Set aside. In a medium saucepan combine the cornstarch, flour and sugar. Gradually stir in the milk and cook over medium heat until thickened and bubbling.

4 In a small bowl, beat the egg yolks lightly. Slowly pour over about 1 cup hot milk into the yolks, stirring constantly. Return yolk mixture to the saucepan and bring to a gentle boil, stirring constantly, until thickened. Stir in the melted white chocolate until well blended. Cool to room temperature, stirring frequently to prevent a skin forming on the surface.

5 In a medium bowl with electric mixer, beat the whipping cream and almond extract until soft peaks form. Fold about ½ cup whipped cream into white chocolate custard and spoon half the custard into the base. Peel and slice mango thinly.

6 Arrange the mango slices over the custard and cover with the remaining custard, smoothing top evenly. Remove side of pan and slide on to serving plate. Spoon remaining cream into large piping bag fitted with a medium star tip. Pipe cream in scroll pattern in parallel rows ½ in apart. Carefully sprinkle chopped toasted almonds between rows.

Chocolate Tiramisú Tart

This version of the famous Italian dessert, tiramisú (or 'pick-me-up') does not contain coffee-soaked biscuits, as they would cause the crust to become soggy.

Serves 12–16

INGREDIENTS
8 tbsp unsalted butter
1 tbsp coffee-flavor liqueur or water
1½ cups flour
¼ cup unsweetened cocoa
¼ cup confectioners' sugar
pinch of salt
¼ tsp vanilla extract
unsweetened cocoa for dusting

CHOCOLATE LAYER
½ cup heavy cream
1 tbsp light corn syrup
4 oz bittersweet chocolate, chopped
2 tbsp unsalted butter, cut into pieces
2 tbsp coffee-flavor liqueur

FILLING
1 cup whipping cream
12 oz mascarpone or cream cheese, at
    room temperature
3 tbsp confectioners' sugar
3 tbsp cold espresso or strong coffee
3 tbsp coffee-flavor liqueur
3½ oz semi-sweet chocolate, grated

1 Prepare pastry. Lightly grease a 9 in springform pan. In a saucepan, heat butter and liqueur or water over medium heat until hot. Into a bowl, sift together flour, cocoa, sugar and salt. Remove butter mixture from the heat, stir in vanilla extract and gradually stir into the flour mixture until a soft dough forms. Knead lightly until smooth. Press on to bottom and up side of pan to within ¾ in of top. Prick dough. Refrigerate for 40 minutes. Preheat oven to 375°F. Bake pastry for 8–10 minutes. If pastry puffs up, prick with fork and bake for 2–3 minutes more until set. Remove to rack to cool.

2 Prepare chocolate layer. In a saucepan over medium heat, bring cream and syrup to a boil. Remove from heat and add chocolate, stirring until melted. Beat in butter and liqueur and pour into the cooked pastry. Cool completely, then refrigerate.

3 Prepare filling. In a bowl with an electric mixer, whip cream until soft peaks form. In another bowl, beat cheese until soft, then beat in sugar until smooth and creamy. Gradually beat in cold coffee and liqueur; gently fold in whipped cream and chocolate. Spoon filling into the chocolate-lined pastry level with the crust. Refrigerate until ready to serve.

mascarpone cheese

bittersweet chocolate

4 To serve, run a sharp knife around the side of the pan to loosen the crust. Unclip the pan side. Sift a layer of cocoa over the tart.

Chocolate Truffle Tart

Any flavor liqueur can be substituted for brandy —
orange, raspberry, coffee and whisky all go very well
with chocolate.

Serves 12

INGREDIENTS
1 cup flour
⅓ cup unsweetened cocoa
 (preferably Dutch-processed)
¼ cup superfine sugar
½ tsp salt
½ cup cold unsalted butter, cut into
 pieces
1 egg yolk
1–2 tbsp iced water
1 oz fine quality white or milk
 chocolate, melted
whipped cream for serving (optional)

TRUFFLE FILLING
1⅓ cups heavy cream
12 oz couverture or fine quality
 bittersweet chocolate, chopped
4 tbsp unsalted butter, cut into pieces
2 tbsp brandy or other liqueur

bittersweet chocolate

milk chocolate

eggs

brandy

cocoa

1 Prepare pastry. Into a small bowl, sift flour and cocoa. In a food processor fitted with metal blade, process flour mixture, sugar and salt to blend. Add butter and process for 15–20 seconds, until mixture resembles coarse crumbs.

2 In a bowl, lightly beat yolk with iced water. Add to flour mixture and using pulse action, process until dough begins to stick together. Turn out dough on to plastic wrap. Use to help shape dough into flat disc and wrap tightly. Refrigerate for 1–2 hours.

Lightly grease a 9 in tart pan with removable base. Soften dough for 5–10 minutes. Roll out dough between sheets of waxed paper or plastic wrap to a 22 in round, about ¼ in thick. Peel off top sheet and invert dough into pan. Remove bottom sheet. Ease dough on to base and side of pan. Prick base with fork. Refrigerate for 1 hour.

Preheat oven to 350°F. Line tart with foil or parchment paper; fill with dried beans. Bake for 5–7 minutes; lift out foil with beans and bake for 5–7 minutes more, until just set. (Pastry may look slightly underdone on bottom but it will dry out.) Remove to rack to cool.

3 Prepare filling. In a medium saucepan over medium heat, bring cream to a boil. Remove pan from heat and stir in chocolate until melted and smooth. Stir in butter and liqueur. Strain into prepared tart pan, tilting slightly to even surface, but do not touch surface.

4 Spoon melted chocolate into a paper cone and cut tip about ¼ in in diameter. Drop rounds of chocolate over surface of tart and with a skewer or toothpick gently draw point through chocolate to produce marbled effect. Refrigerate for 2–3 hours until set. To serve, allow tart to soften slightly at room temperature, about 30 minutes.

Chunky Chocolate Drops

Do not allow these cookies to cool completely on the cookie sheet or they will become too crisp and will break when you try to lift them.

Makes about 18 cookies

INGREDIENTS
6 oz bittersweet or semi-sweet
   chocolate, chopped
½ cup unsalted butter, cut into pieces
2 eggs
½ cup granulated sugar
¼ cup packed light brown sugar
⅓ cup flour
¼ cup unsweetened cocoa
1 tsp baking powder
10 ml/2 tsp vanilla extract
pinch of salt
1 cup pecans, toasted and coarsely
   chopped
1 cup semi-sweet chocolate chips
4 oz fine quality white chocolate,
   chopped into ¼ in pieces
4 oz fine quality milk chocolate,
   chopped into ¼ in pieces

bittersweet chocolate
eggs
cocoa
milk chocolate
white chocolate
pecans

1 Preheat oven to 325°F. Grease 2 large cookie sheets. In a medium saucepan over low heat, melt the bittersweet or semi-sweet chocolate and butter until smooth, stirring frequently. Remove from heat to cool slightly.

2 In a large mixing bowl with electric mixer, beat the eggs and sugars for 2–3 minutes until pale and creamy. Gradually pour in the melted chocolate mixture, beating until well blended. Beat in the flour, cocoa, baking powder, vanilla and salt, until just blended. Stir in the nuts, chocolate chips and chocolate pieces.

3 Drop heaped tablespoons of mixture on to cookie sheets 4 in apart and flatten each to a round about 3 in. (You will only get 4–6 cookies on each sheet.) Bake for 8–10 minutes until tops are shiny and cracked and edges look crisp; do not over-bake or cookies will break when removed from cookie sheet.

4 Remove cookie sheets to wire rack to cool for 2 minutes, until just set, then remove cookies to wire rack to cool completely. Continue to bake in batches. Store in airtight containers.

Chocolate Amaretti

As an alternative decoration, lightly press a few raw sugar crystals on top of each cookie before baking or dust with confectioners' sugar when cold.

Makes about 24

INGREDIENTS
1 cup blanched whole almonds
½ cup superfine sugar
1 tbsp unsweetened cocoa
2 tbsp confectioners' sugar
2 egg whites
pinch of cream of tartar
1 tsp almond extract
slivered almonds to decorate

eggs

cocoa

almonds

almond extract

I Preheat oven to 350°F. Place almonds on a small cookie sheet and bake for 10–12 minutes, stirring occasionally, until almonds are golden brown. Remove from oven and cool to room temperature. Reduce oven temperature to 325°F.

Line a large cookie sheet with parchment paper or foil. In a food processor fitted with a metal blade, process the toasted almonds with ¼ cup sugar until almonds are finely ground but not oily. Transfer to a medium bowl and sift in the cocoa and confectioners' sugar; stir to blend. Set aside.

2 In a medium mixing bowl with electric mixer, beat the egg whites and cream of tartar until stiff peaks form. Sprinkle in remaining ¼ cup sugar a tablespoon at a time, beating well after each addition, and continue beating until whites are glossy and stiff. Beat in almond extract.

3 Sprinkle over almond-sugar mixture and gently fold into beaten egg whites until just blended. Spoon mixture into a large piping bag fitted with a plain ½ in tip. Pipe 1½ in rounds about 1 in apart on prepared cookie sheet. Press a slivered almond into the center of each.

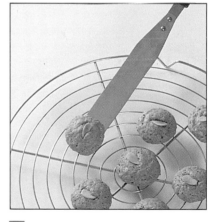

4 Bake cookies for 12–15 minutes or until they appear crisp. Remove cookie sheets to wire rack to cool for 10 minutes. With metal spatula, remove cookies to wire rack to cool completely. When cool, dust with confectioners' sugar and store in an airtight container.

Fudgy Glazed Chocolate Brownies

For a simpler brownie, omit the fudge glaze and dust with confectioners' sugar or cocoa instead.

Serves 8–10

INGREDIENTS

9 oz bittersweet or semi-sweet
  chocolate, chopped
1 oz unsweetened chocolate,
  chopped
½ cup unsalted butter, cut into pieces
½ cup packed dark brown sugar
¼ cup granulated sugar
2 eggs
1 tbsp vanilla extract
½ cup flour
1 cup pecans or walnuts, toasted and
  chopped
5 oz fine quality white chocolate,
  chopped into ¼ in pieces
pecan halves to decorate (optional)

FUDGY CHOCOLATE GLAZE

6 oz semi-sweet or bittersweet
  chocolate, chopped
4 tbsp unsalted butter, cut into pieces
2 tbsp corn syrup
2 tsp vanilla extract
1 tsp instant coffee powder

unsweetened chocolate

white chocolate

pecans

1 Preheat oven to 350°F. Invert an 8 in square baking pan and mold a piece of foil over bottom. Turn pan over and line with molded foil. Lightly grease foil.

2 In a medium saucepan over a low heat, melt the dark chocolates and butter until smooth, stirring frequently. Remove pan from heat.

3 Stir in sugars and continue stirring for 2 more minutes, until sugar has dissolved. Beat in eggs and vanilla and stir in flour just until blended. Stir in pecans and white chocolate. Pour batter into prepared pan.

4 Bake brownies for 20–25 minutes until a toothpick or cake tester inserted 2 in from center comes out with just a few crumbs attached (do not over-bake). Remove pan to a wire rack to cool for 30 minutes. Using the foil as a guide, remove brownies from pan and cool on rack for at least 2 hours.

5 Prepare glaze. In a medium saucepan over medium heat, melt chocolate, butter, syrup, vanilla and coffee powder until smooth, stirring frequently. Remove from heat. Refrigerate for 1 hour or until thickened and spreadable.

6 Invert brownies on to the wire rack, remove foil from bottom. Turn top side up. Using a metal spatula, spread a thick layer of fudgy glaze over top of brownies just to edges. Refrigerate for 1 hour until set. Cut into squares or 'fingers'. If you wish, top each with a pecan half.

Chocolate Crackle-Tops

These cookies are best eaten as fresh as possible, as they dry slightly when stored, but they will last for several days in an airtight container. Pack them in single layers so the tops are not damaged.

Makes about 38 cookies

INGREDIENTS
7 oz bittersweet or semi-sweet
    chocolate, chopped
7 tbsp unsalted butter
²⁄₃ cup superfine sugar
3 eggs
1 tsp vanilla extract
1½ cups flour
¼ cup unsweetened cocoa
½ tsp baking powder
pinch of salt
1½ cups confectioners' sugar for
    coating

eggs

vanilla extract

bittersweet
chocolate

1 Prepare dough. In a medium saucepan over low heat, heat the chocolate and butter until smooth, stirring frequently. Remove from heat. Stir in sugar, continue stirring for 2–3 minutes until sugar dissolves. Add eggs one at a time, beating well after each addition; stir in vanilla. Into a bowl, sift together flour, cocoa, baking powder and salt. Gradually stir into the chocolate mixture in batches, just until blended. Cover dough and refrigerate for at least 1 hour until dough is cold and holds its shape.

2 Preheat oven to 325°F. Grease 2 or more large cookie sheets. Place confectioners' sugar in a small, deep bowl. Using a small ice-cream scoop (about 1 in diameter) or round teaspoon, scoop cold dough into small balls and, between palms of hands, roll into 1½ in balls.

3 Drop balls one at a time into confectioners' sugar and roll until heavily coated. Remove ball with a slotted spoon and tap against side of bowl to remove excess sugar. Place on cookie sheets 1½ in apart. Use more sugar as necessary. (You may need to recycle the cookie sheets.)

4 Bake cookies for 10–15 minutes or until top of cookie feels slightly firm when touched with fingertip (do not over-bake or cookies will be dry). Remove cookie sheet to wire rack for 2–3 minutes, until just set. With a metal spatula remove cookies to wire rack to cool completely.

Chocolate Blueberry Muffins

Paper liners not only make for easier washing up, but keep the muffins fresher.

Makes 12

INGREDIENTS
½ cup butter
3 oz unsweetened chocolate, chopped
1 cup granulated sugar
1 egg, lightly beaten
1 cup buttermilk
2 tsp vanilla extract
2 cups flour
1 tsp baking soda
1 cup fresh or frozen blueberries, thawed
1 oz bittersweet chocolate, melted

bittersweet chocolate

eggs

vanilla extract

unsweetened chocolate

blueberries

1 Preheat oven to 375°F. In a medium saucepan over medium heat, melt the butter and chocolate until smooth, stirring frequently. Remove from heat to cool slightly.

2 Stir in the sugar, egg, buttermilk and vanilla extract. Gently fold in the flour and baking soda until just blended. (Do not overblend; the mixture may be lumpy with some unblended flour.) Fold in the berries.

3 Spoon batter into 12 greased or paper-lined 2½ in muffin cups, filling to the top. Bake for 25–30 minutes until a skewer inserted in the center comes out with just a few crumbs attached. Remove muffins in their paper liners to wire rack immediately (if left in the pan they will go soggy). Drizzle with the melted chocolate and serve warm or cool.

Chocolate Raspberry Macaroon Bars

Any seedless preserve, such as strawberry or apricot, can be substituted for raspberry.

Makes 16–18 bars

INGREDIENTS
½ cup unsalted butter, softened
½ cup confectioners' sugar
⅓ cup unsweetened cocoa
   (preferably Dutch-processed)
pinch of salt
1 tsp almond extract
1 cup flour

TOPPING
½ cup seedless raspberry preserve
1 tbsp raspberry-flavor liqueur
1 cup mini chocolate chips
1½ cups finely ground almonds
4 egg whites
pinch of salt
1 cup superfine sugar
½ tsp almond extract
⅓ cup slivered almonds

raspberry preserve

eggs

chocolate chips

1 Preheat oven to 325°F. Invert a 9 × 13 in baking pan. Mold a sheet of foil over pan and smooth foil evenly around corners. Lift off foil and turn pan right side up; line with molded foil. Grease foil.

2 In a medium bowl with an electric mixer, beat together the butter, sugar, cocoa and salt until well blended, about 1 minute. Beat in the almond extract and the flour until mixture forms a crumbly dough.

3 Turn dough into the prepared pan and pat firmly over bottom to make an even layer. Prick dough with a fork. Bake for 20 minutes until just set. Remove from oven and increase temperature to 375°F.

4 In a small bowl, combine the raspberry preserve and raspberry-flavor liqueur. Spread evenly over chocolate crust, then sprinkle evenly with the chocolate chips.

5 In a food processor fitted with a metal blade, process the almonds, egg whites, salt, sugar and almond extract until well blended and foamy. Gently pour over jam layer, spreading evenly to edges of pan. Sprinkle with slivered almonds.

6 Bake for 20–25 minutes more until top is golden and puffed. Remove to wire rack to cool in pan for 20 minutes or until firm. Using edges of foil, carefully remove from pan and cool completely. Peel off foil and, using a sharp knife, cut into bars.

Black and White Ginger Florentines

These florentines can be refrigerated in an airtight container for one week.

Makes about 30

INGREDIENTS
½ cup heavy cream
¼ cup unsalted butter
½ cup granulated sugar
2 tbsp honey
1⅔ cups slivered almonds
⅓ cup flour
½ tsp ground ginger
⅓ cup diced candied orange peel
½ cup diced stem ginger
2 oz semi-sweet chocolate, chopped
5 oz bittersweet chocolate, chopped
5 oz fine quality white chocolate, chopped

bittersweet chocolate

honey

candied orange peel

white chocolate

slivered almonds

1 Preheat oven to 350°F. Lightly grease 2 large cookie sheets. (Non-stick sheets are ideal for these caramel-like cookies.) In a medium saucepan over medium heat, stir cream, butter, sugar and honey until sugar dissolves. Bring mixture to the boil, stirring constantly. Remove from heat and stir in almonds, flour and ground ginger until well blended. Stir in orange peel, stem ginger and chopped semi-sweet chocolate.

2 Drop teaspoons of mixture on to prepared sheets at least 3 in apart. Spread each round as thinly as possible with the back of the spoon. (Dip spoon into water to prevent sticking.)

3 Bake for 8–10 minutes or until edges are golden brown and cookies are bubbling. Do not underbake or they will be sticky, but be careful not to over-bake as the high sugar and fat content allows them to burn easily. Continue baking in batches. If you wish, use a 3 in cookie cutter to neaten the edges of the florentines while on the cookie sheet.

4 Remove to wire rack to cool for 10 minutes until firm. Using a metal spatula, carefully remove cookies to wire rack to cool completely.

5 In a small saucepan over very low heat, heat the bittersweet chocolate, stirring frequently, until melted and smooth. Cool slightly. In the top of a double boiler over low heat, melt the white chocolate until smooth, stirring frequently. Remove top of double boiler from bottom and cool for about 5 minutes, stirring occasionally until slightly thickened.

6 Using a small metal spatula, spread half the florentines with the bittersweet chocolate on flat side of each cookie, swirling to create a decorative surface, and place on wire rack, chocolate side up. Spread remaining florentines with the melted white chocolate and place on rack, chocolate side up. Refrigerate for 10–15 minutes to set completely.

White Chocolate Brownies with Milk Chocolate Macadamia Topping

If you wish, hazelnuts can be substituted for the macadamia nuts in the topping.

Serves 12

INGREDIENTS
1 cup flour
½ tsp baking powder
pinch of salt
6 oz fine quality white chocolate, chopped
½ cup superfine sugar
½ cup unsalted butter, cut into pieces
2 eggs, lightly beaten
1 tsp vanilla extract
6 oz semi-sweet chocolate chips or semi-sweet chocolate, chopped

TOPPING
7 oz milk chocolate, chopped
1 cup unsalted macadamia nuts, chopped

milk chocolate

macadamia nuts

1 Preheat oven to 350°F. Grease a 9 in springform pan. Sift together the flour, baking powder and salt, set aside.

2 In a medium saucepan over medium heat, melt the white chocolate, sugar and butter until smooth, stirring frequently. Cool slightly, then beat in the eggs and vanilla. Stir in the flour until well blended. Stir in the chocolate chips or chopped chocolate. Spread evenly in the prepared pan, smoothing top.

3 Bake for 20–25 minutes until a toothpick inserted 2 in from side of pan comes out clean; do not over-bake. Remove from the oven to a heatproof surface. Immediately sprinkle chopped milk chocolate evenly over surface (avoid touching the side of pan) and return to oven for 1 minute.

4 Remove from oven and, using the back of a spoon, gently spread the softened chocolate evenly over the top. Sprinkle with the macadamias and gently press into chocolate. Cool on wire rack 30 minutes, then refrigerate until set, about 1 hour. Run a sharp knife around the side of the pan to loosen; then unclip springform pan side and carefully remove. Cut into thin wedges.

Chocolate-dipped Hazelnut Crescents

Walnuts or pecans can be used instead of hazelnuts, but they must be finely ground.

Makes about 35

INGREDIENTS
2 cups flour
pinch of salt
1 cup unsalted butter, softened
⅓ cup superfine sugar
1 tbsp hazelnut liqueur or water
1 tsp vanilla extract
½ cup semi-sweet chocolate, finely
    grated
½ cup hazelnuts, toasted and finely
    chopped
confectioners' sugar for dusting
12 oz semi-sweet chocolate, melted,
    for dipping

*semi-sweet
chocolate*

hazelnuts

vanilla extract

I Preheat oven to 325°F. Grease 2 large cookie sheets. Sift the flour and salt into a bowl.

2 In a large bowl with an electric mixer, beat the butter until creamy, about 1 minute. Add the sugar and beat until fluffy, beat in the hazelnut liqueur and vanilla. Gently stir in the flour, until just blended, then fold in the grated chocolate and hazelnuts.

3 With floured hands, shape the dough into 2 × ½ in crescent shapes. Place on cookie sheets, 2 in apart. Bake for 20–25 minutes until edges are set and the cookies slightly golden. Remove cookie sheets to rack to cool for 10 minutes. Transfer cookies from cookie sheets to racks to cool completely.

4 Dust cookies with confectioners' sugar. Using a pair of kitchen tongs or fingers dip half of each crescent into melted chocolate. Place on waxed paper-lined cookie sheet and cool. Chill until chocolate sets.

Chocolate Soufflé Crêpes

A non-stick pan is ideal as it does not need greasing between each crêpe. Serve two crêpes per person.

Makes 12 crêpes

INGREDIENTS
7 tbsp flour
1 tbsp unsweetened cocoa
1 tsp superfine sugar
pinch of salt
1 tsp ground cinnamon
2 eggs
¾ cup milk
1 tsp vanilla extract
4 tbsp unsalted butter, melted
confectioners' sugar for dusting
raspberries, pineapple and mint sprigs
　　to decorate

PINEAPPLE SYRUP
½ medium pineapple, peeled, cored
　　and finely chopped
½ cup water
2 tbsp natural maple syrup
1 tsp cornstarch
½ cinnamon stick
2 tbsp rum

SOUFFLÉ FILLING
9 oz semi-sweet or bittersweet
　　chocolate
⅓ cup heavy cream
3 eggs, separated
2 tbsp superfine sugar

mint sprigs

*bittersweet
chocolate*

cinnamon stick　　*raspberries*

1 Prepare syrup. In a saucepan over medium heat, bring pineapple, water, maple syrup, cornstarch and cinnamon stick to the boil. Simmer for 2–3 minutes until sauce thickens, whisking frequently. Remove from heat; discard cinnamon. Pour into a bowl, stir in rum and chill.

4 Prepare filling. In a small saucepan, over medium heat, melt chocolate and cream until smooth, stirring frequently.

2 Prepare crêpes. In a bowl, sift flour, cocoa, sugar, salt and cinnamon. Stir to blend, then make a well in the center. In a bowl, beat eggs, milk and vanilla and gradually add to the well in the flour mixture, whisking in flour from the side of the bowl to form a smooth batter. Stir in half the melted butter and pour batter into a pitcher. Allow to stand 1 hour.

5 In a bowl, with electric mixer, beat yolks with half the sugar for 3–5 minutes, until light and creamy. Gradually beat in the chocolate mixture. Allow to cool. In a large bowl with cleaned beaters, beat egg whites until soft peaks form. Gradually beat in remaining sugar until stiff peaks form. Beat in a large spoonful of whites to the chocolate mixture to lighten it, then fold in remaining whites.

3 Heat a 7–8 in crêpe pan. Brush with butter. Stir the batter. Pour 3 tbsp batter into the pan; swirl pan quickly to cover bottom with a thin layer. Cook over medium-high heat for 1–2 minutes until bottom is golden. Turn over and cook for 30–45 seconds, then turn on to a plate.
　　Stack crêpes between waxed paper and set aside.

6 Preheat oven to 400°F. Lay a crêpe on a plate, bottom side up. Spoon on a little soufflé mixture, spreading it to the edge. Fold the bottom half over the soufflé mixture, then fold in half again to form a filled 'triangle'. Place on a buttered cookie sheet. Repeat with remaining crêpes. Brush the tops with melted butter and bake for 15–20 minutes until filling has souffléd. Garnish with mint and a spoonful of syrup.

Luxury Mocha Mousse

As a variation, use an orange-flavor liqueur, brandy or even water in place of the coffee.

Serves 6

INGREDIENTS
8 oz fine quality bittersweet
    chocolate, chopped
¼ cup espresso or strong coffee
2 tbsp butter, cut into pieces
2 tbsp brandy or rum
3 eggs, separated
pinch of salt
3 tbsp superfine sugar
½ cup whipping cream
2 tbsp coffee-flavor liqueur
chocolate coffee beans to decorate
    (optional)

bittersweet chocolate

eggs

chocolate coffee beans

1 In a medium saucepan over medium heat, melt the chocolate and coffee, stirring frequently until smooth. Remove from the heat and beat in the butter and brandy or rum.

2 In a small bowl, beat the yolks lightly then beat into the melted chocolate; the mixture will thicken. Cool. In a large bowl with electric mixer, beat the whites to 'break' them. Add a pinch of salt and beat on medium speed until soft peaks form. Increase speed and beat until stiff peaks form. Beat in sugar, 1 tbsp at a time, beating well after each addition until whites are glossy and stiff, but not dry.

3 Beat 1 large spoonful of whites into chocolate mixture to lighten it, then fold chocolate into remaining whites. Pour into a large glass serving bowl or 6 individual dishes and refrigerate for at least 3–4 hours before serving.

4 In a medium bowl, beat the cream and coffee-flavor liqueur until soft peaks form. Spoon into a piping bag fitted with medium star tip and pipe rosettes or shells on to surface of mousse. Garnish with a chocolate coffee bean.

Chocolate Pavlova with Chocolate Curls and Fruits

Do not attempt to make meringues on a hot humid day, as the moisture can make the meringue go sticky or 'weep'.

Serves 8–10

INGREDIENTS
2¼ cups confectioners' sugar
1 tbsp unsweetened cocoa
1 tsp cornstarch
5 egg whites at room temperature
pinch of salt
1 tsp cider vinegar or lemon juice

CHOCOLATE CREAM
6 oz bittersweet or semi-sweet
   chocolate, chopped
½ cup milk
2 tbsp unsalted butter, cut into pieces
2 tbsp brandy
2 cups heavy or whipping cream

TOPPING
chocolate curls to decorate
2 cups mixed berries or cut-up fruits
   such as mango, papaya, fresh
   lychees and pineapple
confectioners' sugar to decorate

bittersweet chocolate

eggs

mixed berries

1 Prepare meringue. Preheat oven to 325°F. Place a sheet of parchment paper on a cookie sheet and mark an 8 in circle on it. In a small bowl, sift together 3 tbsp confectioners' sugar, with the cocoa and cornstarch. In a mixing bowl with electric mixer, beat egg whites until frothy. Add salt and beat until whites form stiff peaks. Sprinkle in the remaining confectioners' sugar, a little at a time, making sure each addition is dissolved before adding the next. Fold in sugar mixture; then quickly fold in vinegar or lemon juice.

2 Spoon the mixture on to the circle on the paper, building up the sides higher than the center. Bake in the center of the oven for 1 hour until set. Turn off oven and allow the meringue to stand in the oven for 1 hour longer (the meringue may crack or sink). Remove from oven and cool.

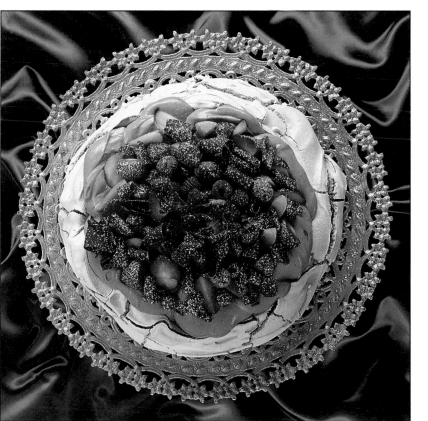

3 Prepare the chocolate cream. In a medium saucepan over low heat, melt the chocolate and milk, stirring until smooth. Remove from the heat and whisk in the butter and brandy and cool for 1 hour.

4 Using a metal spatula, transfer meringue to a serving plate. Cut a circle around the center of the meringue about 2 in from the edge to allow the center to sink without pulling edges in. When chocolate mixture has cooled, but is not too firm, in a medium bowl with electric mixer beat the cream until soft peaks form. Stir half the cream into the chocolate to lighten it, then fold in remaining cream. Spoon into the center of the meringue. Arrange chocolate curls and fruit in the center of the meringue, over the cream. Dust with confectioners' sugar.

Hazelnut Chocolate Meringue Torte with Pears

Do not assemble this torte more than 3–4 hours before serving, as the pears may give off liquid and soften the cream too much.

Serves 8–10

INGREDIENTS
¾ cup granulated sugar
1 vanilla pod, split
2 cups water
4 ripe pears, peeled, halved and cored
2 tbsp pear or hazelnut-flavor liqueur
1¼ cups hazelnuts, toasted
6 egg whites
pinch of salt
2½ cups confectioners' sugar
1 tsp vanilla extract
2 oz semi-sweet chocolate, melted

CHOCOLATE FILLING
10 oz fine quality bittersweet or semi-sweet chocolate, chopped
2 cups whipping cream
¼ cup pear or hazelnut-flavor liqueur

bittersweet chocolate

eggs

hazelnut-flavor liqueur

pears

hazelnuts

1 In a saucepan large enough to hold the pears in a single layer combine sugar, vanilla pod and water. Over high heat, bring to a boil, stirring until sugar dissolves. Reduce heat to medium. Lower pears into the syrup. Cover pears and simmer gently for 12–15 minutes until tender. Remove pan from heat and allow pears to cool in their poaching liquid. Carefully remove pears from liquid. Place on a flat plate lined with layers of paper towel. Sprinkle each half with the liqueur. Cover and refrigerate overnight.

4 Prepare chocolate cream. Place chocolate in a small bowl. Set bowl over a pan of simmering water, turn off heat. Stir chocolate until melted and smooth. Cool chocolate to room temperature. In a bowl with electric mixer, beat cream to soft peaks. Quickly fold cream into melted chocolate; fold in liqueur. Spoon about one-third of chocolate cream into a piping bag fitted with a star tip. Set aside.

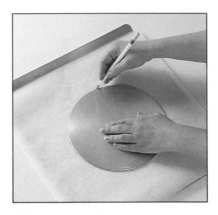

2 Preheat oven to 350°F. With a pencil draw a 9 in circle in the center of each of 2 sheets of parchment paper or well greased foil. Turn paper over on to 2 cookie sheets (so pencil marks are underneath) or slide foil on to cookie sheets. In a food processor fitted with metal blade, process the toasted hazelnuts until medium-fine crumbs form.

3 In a large bowl with an electric mixer on medium, beat the whites until frothy. Add salt and beat on high speed until soft peaks form. Reduce mixer speed and gradually add sugar, beating well after each addition until all the sugar is added and whites are stiff and glossy; this takes 12–15 minutes. Gently fold in nuts and vanilla and spoon meringue on to cookie sheets, spreading into 9 in circles, smoothing top and sides. Bake for 1 hour until tops are dry and firm. Turn off oven and allow to cool in the oven, 2–3 hours or overnight, until completely dry.

5 To assemble, with a sharp knife, thinly slice each pear half lengthwise. Place one meringue layer on a serving plate. Spread with half the chocolate cream and arrange half the sliced pears evenly over the cream. Pipe a border of rosettes around the edge.

6 Top with the second meringue layer and spread with the remaining chocolate cream. Arrange the remaining pear slices in an attractive pattern over the chocolate cream. Pipe a border of rosettes around the edge. Spoon the melted chocolate into a small paper cone and drizzle the chocolate over the pears. Refrigerate for at least 1 hour before serving.

White Chocolate Hearts with Two Sauces

The caramel nests should not be made more than a few hours before serving, as the sugar begins to soften fairly quickly.

Serves 6

INGREDIENTS
1 ⅓ cups whipping cream
4 oz fine quality white chocolate, chopped
⅔ package unflavored gelatin
¼ cup water
1 cup water
4 egg yolks
¼ cup granulated sugar
2 tbsp orange-flavor liqueur
4 small mandarin oranges or tangerines, peeled and sectioned
6 kumquats, thinly sliced

CARAMEL SAUCE
1 ⅓ cup granulated sugar
1 ⅓ cup water

CHOCOLATE SAUCE
8 oz fine quality bittersweet chocolate, chopped
¼ cup unsalted butter, cut into pieces
¾ cup water
2 tbsp brandy or chocolate-flavor liqueur

CARAMEL NESTS (OPTIONAL)
4 oz granulated sugar
¼ cup water
2 tbsp corn syrup

bittersweet chocolate

kumquats

tangerines

white chocolate

eggs

1 Lightly oil 6 × ½ cup heart-shaped or other molds. In a small saucepan over low heat, bring ⅓ cup cream to a boil. Add the white chocolate all at once, stirring constantly until smooth. Set aside. Sprinkle gelatin over water in a small bowl; allow to stand and soften.

2 In a medium saucepan over medium heat, bring milk to a boil. In a medium bowl with a hand-held electric mixer, beat the egg yolks and sugar until thick and pale, 2–3 minutes. Reduce mixer to lowest speed; gradually beat in milk, then return custard mixture to saucepan.

3 Cook custard over medium heat, stirring constantly with a wooden spoon until mixture thickens slightly and coats the back of the spoon. (Do not boil or custard will curdle.) Remove from the heat and stir in softened gelatin until completely dissolved; then stir into the chocolate mixture. Strain custard into a large chilled pitcher. Stir in orange-flavored liqueur and refrigerate for about 20 minutes until mixture begins to thicken, stirring occasionally.

4 In a mixing bowl with electric mixer, beat remaining 1 cup cream until soft peaks form. Gently fold into the thickening custard mixture. Carefully pour into molds. Place molds on cookie sheet and refrigerate for 2 hours or until set. Cover molds with plastic wrap and refrigerate for several hours or overnight. (Unmold desserts at least 30 minutes before serving to soften slightly.)
Prepare caramel sauce. Place sugar and

half the water into a heavy-bottomed saucepan. Stir over medium heat until sugar dissolves. Increase heat and boil, swirling pan occasionally until syrup turns light brown, 3–4 minutes. Remove from heat and, standing back from pan, pour in remaining water (mixture will spit). Return to heat and simmer gently until caramel dissolves, stirring occasionally. Cool then pour into serving bowl and keep at room temperature.

5 Prepare chocolate sauce. In medium saucepan over medium heat, melt the chocolate, butter and water until smooth, stirring frequently. Remove from heat and cool slightly. Stir in brandy or liqueur and strain into serving bowl; cool to room temperature. (Sauce can be made ahead, but may solidify if refrigerated. Heat gently then cool before serving.)

6 To serve, fill a pie plate or soup bowl with hot water. Run a sharp knife around the edge of each mold and dip into the hot water for 4–6 seconds. Dry bottom of mold; quickly cover dessert with a plate. Invert mold on to plate, giving a firm shake; carefully remove mold. Spoon a little of each sauce around each heart-shaped cream and arrange fruits on plates. If you like, garnish with caramel nests and serve with additional sauce.

CARAMEL NESTS

Wrap a rolling pin in foil and brush lightly with oil. Place on a lightly oiled cookie sheet. Tape together 2 long tined forks.

In a small heavy-based saucepan over medium heat, swirl the sugar and water until dissolved. Bring to the boil and add the syrup, swirl to blend. Half cover the pan and boil until the syrup turns a light caramel brown, about 3–4 minutes. Immediately dip the base of the pan into ice cold water to stop cooking.

Dip the forks into the caramel and holding the rolling pin over the cookie sheet, sharply flick the fork backwards and forwards over the pin to form long, thin strands of sugar. Repeat by dipping forks with syrup and flicking. Cut spun sugar into pieces and mold over dessert plates.

Chocolate Amaretto Marquise

A 9 in springform cake pan is ideal for this recipe, but for special occasions it is worth taking extra time to line a heart-shaped pan carefully.

Serves 10–12

INGREDIENTS

1 tbsp flavorless vegetable oil, such as sunflower
7–8 amaretti biscuits, finely crushed
2 tbsp unblanched almonds, toasted and finely chopped
1 lb fine quality bittersweet or semi-sweet chocolate, broken into pieces or chopped
⅓ cup Amaretto liqueur
⅓ cup corn syrup
2 cups heavy cream
unsweetened cocoa for dusting

AMARETTO CREAM (OPTIONAL)

1½ cups whipping or heavy cream for serving
2–3 tbsp Amaretto liqueur

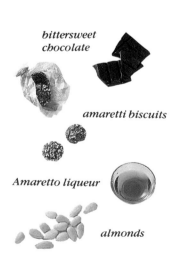

bittersweet chocolate

amaretti biscuits

Amaretto liqueur

almonds

1 Lightly oil a 9 in heart-shaped or springform cake pan. Line the bottom with parchment paper and oil the paper. In a small bowl, combine the crushed amaretti biscuits and the chopped almonds. Sprinkle evenly on to the bottom of the pan.

2 Place the chocolate, Amaretto liqueur and corn syrup in a medium saucepan over a very low heat. Stir frequently until chocolate is melted and mixture is smooth. Allow to cool until mixture feels just warm to the touch, about 6–8 minutes.

3 In a bowl with electric mixer, beat the cream until it just begins to hold its shape. Stir in a large spoonful to the chocolate mixture, then add quickly remaining cream and gently fold into the chocolate mixture. Pour into the prepared pan and tap pan gently on the work surface to release any large air bubbles. Cover the pan with plastic wrap and refrigerate overnight.

4 To unmold, run a thin-bladed sharp knife under hot water and dry carefully. Run the knife around the edge of the pan to loosen dessert. Place a serving plate over the pan, then invert to unmold the dessert. Carefully peel off the paper, replacing any crust that sticks to it, and dust with cocoa. To serve, whip the cream and Amaretto liqueur until soft peaks form and serve separately.

Double Chocolate Snowball

This is an ideal party dessert as it can be prepared at least one day ahead and decorated on the day.

Serves 12–14

INGREDIENTS

12 oz bittersweet or semi-sweet
   chocolate, chopped
1½ cups superfine sugar
1¼ cups unsalted butter, cut into
   small pieces
8 eggs
¼ cup orange-flavored liqueur or
   brandy (optional)
cocoa for dusting

WHITE CHOCOLATE CREAM

7 oz fine quality white chocolate,
   broken into pieces
2 cups heavy or whipping cream
1 tbsp orange-flavor liqueur
   (optional)

bittersweet chocolate

eggs

white chocolate

1 Preheat the oven to 350°F. Line a 1½ quart round ovenproof bowl with aluminum foil, smoothing the sides. In a bowl over a pan of simmering water, melt the bittersweet or semi-sweet chocolate. Add sugar and stir until chocolate is melted and sugar dissolves. Strain into a medium bowl. With an electric mixer at low speed, beat in the butter, then the eggs, one at a time, beating well after each addition. Stir in the liqueur or brandy and pour into the prepared bowl. Tap gently to release any large air bubbles.

2 Bake for 1¼–1½ hours until the surface is firm and slightly risen, but cracked. The center will still be wobbly: this will set on cooling. Remove to rack to cool to room temperature; the top will sink. Cover with a dinner plate (to make an even surface for unmolding); then cover completely with clear film or foil and refrigerate overnight. To unmold, remove plate and film or foil and place a serving plate over the top of the mold. Invert mold on to plate and shake firmly to release the dessert. Carefully peel off foil. Cover until ready to decorate.

3 In a food processor fitted with a metal blade, process the white chocolate until fine crumbs form. In a small saucepan, heat ½ cup cream until just beginning to simmer. With the food processor running, pour cream through the feed tube and process until the chocolate is completely melted. Strain into a medium bowl and cool to room temperature, stirring occasionally.

4 In another bowl, with the electric mixer, beat the cream and chocolate mixture until soft peaks form, add liqueur and beat for 30 seconds or until cream holds its shape, but not until stiff. Fold a spoonful of cream into the chocolate mixture to lighten it, then fold in remaining cream. Spoon into a piping bag fitted with a star tip and pipe rosettes over the surface. If you wish, dust with cocoa.

White Chocolate Raspberry Ripple Ice Cream

Freeze ice cream in a soufflé dish or other attractive bowl so it can be served directly at the table.

Makes 1¾ pints

INGREDIENTS
1 cup milk
2 cups whipping cream
7 egg yolks
2 tbsp granulated sugar
8 oz fine quality white chocolate, chopped
1 tsp vanilla extract
mint sprigs to decorate

RASPBERRY RIPPLE SAUCE
10 oz packet frozen raspberries in light syrup or 10 oz jar reduced sugar raspberry preserve
2 tsp corn syrup
1 tbsp lemon juice
1 tbsp cornstarch diluted in 1 tbsp water

raspberries

eggs

white chocolate

lemon juice

1 Prepare sauce. Press raspberries and their syrup through a sieve into a saucepan. Add corn syrup, lemon juice and dissolved cornstarch. (If using preserve, omit cornstarch, but add the water.) Bring to a boil, stirring frequently, and simmer for 1–2 minutes until syrupy. Pour into a bowl and cool, then refrigerate.

2 In a pan, combine milk and 1 cup cream and bring to a boil. In a bowl with a hand-held mixer, beat yolks and sugar until thick and creamy, 2–3 minutes. Gradually pour hot milk over yolks and return to pan. Cook over medium heat until custard coats back of a wooden spoon, stirring constantly. (Do not boil or custard will curdle.)

3 Remove pan from heat and stir in the white chocolate until melted and smooth. Pour remaining cream into a large bowl. Strain the hot custard into bowl with cream and vanilla. Blend well and cool to room temperature. Refrigerate until cold. Transfer custard to an ice cream maker and freeze according to manufacturer's instructions.

4 When mixture is frozen, but still soft, transfer one-third of the ice cream to a bowl. Spoon over some raspberry sauce. Cover with another third of the ice cream and more sauce. Cover with remaining ice cream and more sauce. With a knife or spoon, lightly marble sauce into the ice cream. Cover and freeze. Allow ice cream to soften for 20–30 minutes in the refrigerator before serving with remaining raspberry sauce.

French-style Coupe Glacée with Chocolate Ice Cream

This dessert can be made with a good quality bought ice cream, but this extra rich chocolate ice cream is the main feature.

Serves 6–8

INGREDIENTS
8 oz bittersweet chocolate, chopped
1 cup milk mixed with 1 cup light cream
3 egg yolks
¼ cup granulated sugar
1½ cups heavy cream
1 tbsp vanilla extract
chocolate triangles to decorate

ESPRESSO CREAM
3 tbsp instant espresso powder, dissolved in 3 tbsp boiling water, cooled
1½ cups heavy cream
2 tbsp coffee-flavor liqueur

CHOCOLATE ESPRESSO SAUCE
1¼ cups heavy cream
2 tbsp instant espresso powder, dissolved in 3 tbsp boiling water
11 oz bittersweet chocolate, chopped
2 tbsp coffee-flavor liqueur

bittersweet chocolate

espresso powder

1 Prepare ice cream. In a saucepan over a low heat, melt the chocolate with ½ cup of milk mixture, stirring frequently. Remove from heat. In a saucepan over medium heat, bring to a boil remaining milk mixture. In a mixing bowl with a hand-held mixer, beat yolks and sugar until thick and creamy, 2–3 minutes. Gradually pour hot milk mixture over yolks, whisking constantly, and return mixture to pan. Cook over medium heat until custard thickens, stirring constantly. (Do not boil or custard will curdle.) Immediately pour over melted chocolate, stirring until blended.

2 Pour cream into a bowl and strain custard into bowl with vanilla. Blend and cool to room temperature. Refrigerate until cold. Transfer to an ice cream maker and freeze according to instructions.

3 Meanwhile, prepare espresso cream. In a large bowl stir the cooled, dissolved espresso powder into the cream. With an electric mixer, beat the cream until it holds soft peaks. Beat in the liqueur and beat for 30 seconds longer. Spoon cream into a piping bag fitted with a medium star tip and refrigerate until ready to assemble dessert.

4 Prepare sauce. In a saucepan over medium heat, bring cream and dissolved espresso powder to a boil. Remove from heat and add chocolate all at once. Stir until chocolate melts. Add liqueur and strain into a bowl. Keep warm. To serve, soften ice cream for 15–20 minutes at room temperature. Pipe a layer of espresso cream into the bottom of six large wine goblets. Add scoops of ice cream. Spoon over warm chocolate sauce and top with rosette of cream. Serve with remaining sauce.

SWEETS AND CANDIES

Chocolate Truffles

Truffles can be simply dusted with cocoa, confectioners' sugar, finely chopped nuts or coated in melted chocolate.

Makes 20 large or 30 medium truffles

INGREDIENTS
1 cup heavy cream
10 oz fine quality bittersweet or semi-
   sweet chocolate, chopped
3 tbsp unsalted butter, cut into small
   pieces
3 tbsp brandy, whisky or other liqueur

TO FINISH (OPTIONAL)
unsweetened cocoa for dusting
finely chopped pistachios
14 oz bittersweet chocolate

bittersweet chocolate

brandy

pistachios

cocoa

1 In a saucepan over medium heat, bring cream to a boil. Remove from heat and add chocolate all at once. Stir gently until melted. Stir in butter until melted, then stir in brandy or liqueur. Strain into a bowl and cool to room temperature. Cover and refrigerate for 4 hours or overnight.

4 Alternatively, roll in very finely chopped pistachios. Refrigerate for up to 10 days or freeze for up to 2 months.

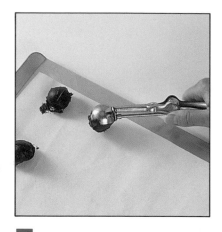

2 Using a small ice cream scoop, melon baller or tablespoon, scrape up mixture into 20 large balls or 30 medium balls and place on a wax paper-lined cookie sheet.

3 If dusting with cocoa, sift a thick layer of cocoa on to a dish or pie plate. Roll truffles in cocoa, rounding them between the palms of your hands.'(Dust your hands with cocoa to prevent truffles sticking.) Do not worry if the truffles are not perfectly round as the irregular shape looks more authentic.

5 If coating with chocolate, do not roll in cocoa or nuts, but freeze for 1 hour. Temper the chocolate. Alternatively, truffles can be coated with chocolate melted by the direct heat method if refrigerated immediately. In a small bowl, melt chocolate by either method. Using a fork, dip truffles into melted chocolate, one at a time, tapping fork on edge of bowl to shake off excess. Place on a parchment paper or waxed paper-lined baking sheet. If chocolate begins to thicken, reheat gently until smooth. Refrigerate until set.

Chocolate Fudge Ribbon

This fudge can be stored in an airtight container in the fridge for up to two weeks.

Makes about 48 triangles

INGREDIENTS
1 lb 5 oz fine quality white chocolate, chopped
14 fl oz can sweetened condensed milk
1 tbsp vanilla extract
1 ½ tsp freshly squeezed lemon juice
pinch of salt
1 ½ cups hazelnuts or pecans, chopped (optional)
6 oz semi-sweet chocolate, chopped
3 tbsp unsalted butter, cut into pieces
2 oz semi-sweet chocolate, melted, for drizzling

semi-sweet chocolate

vanilla extract

lemon

white chocolate

hazelnuts

1 Line an 8 in square baking pan with foil. Oil bottom and sides of foil. In a saucepan over low heat, melt chocolate and condensed milk until smooth, stirring frequently. Remove from heat and stir in vanilla extract, lemon juice and salt; if using, stir in nuts. Spread half the mixture in the pan. Refrigerate for 15 minutes.

2 In a saucepan over low heat, melt chocolate and butter until smooth, stirring frequently. Remove from heat, cool slightly, then pour over chilled white layer and refrigerate for 15 minutes.

3 Gently re-heat remaining white chocolate mixture and pour over set chocolate layer, smooth top, then refrigerate until set, 2–4 hours.

4 Using foil as a guide, remove fudge from pan and turn on to cutting board. Remove foil and with a sharp knife cut into 24 squares. Cut each square into triangles. If you wish, drizzle with melted chocolate.

Chocolate Peppermint Crisps

If you do not have a sugar thermometer, test cooked sugar for 'hard ball stage' by spooning a few drops into a bowl of cold water; it should form a hard ball when rolled between fingers.

Makes 30 crisps

INGREDIENTS
¼ cup granulated sugar
¼ cup water
1 tsp peppermint extract
8 oz bittersweet or semi-sweet
  chocolate, chopped

bittersweet chocolate

peppermint extract

1 Lightly brush a large cookie sheet with flavorless oil. In a saucepan over medium heat, heat the sugar and water, swirling pan gently until sugar dissolves. Boil rapidly until sugar reaches 280°F on a sugar thermometer (see introduction). Remove pan from heat and add peppermint extract; swirl to blend. Pour on to the cookie sheet and allow to set and cool completely.

2 When cold, break into small pieces. Place in a food processor fitted with the metal blade and process until fine crumbs form; do not over-process.

3 Line 2 cookie sheets with parchment paper or waxed paper. Place chocolate in a small bowl over a small saucepan of hot water. Place over very low heat until chocolate has melted, stirring frequently until smooth. Remove from heat and stir in peppermint mixture.

4 Using a teaspoon, drop small mounds on to prepared sheets. Using the back of the spoon, spread to 1½ in rounds. Cool, then refrigerate to set for about 1 hour. Peel off the paper and store in airtight containers with waxed paper between the layers.

Chocolate Nut Clusters

If you do not possess a sugar thermometer, you can test cooked sugar for 'soft ball stage' by spooning a small amount into a bowl of cold water: it should form a soft ball when rolled between finger and thumb.

Makes about 30

INGREDIENTS
2¼ cups heavy cream
2 tbsp unsalted butter, cut into small pieces
1½ cups corn syrup
1 cup granulated sugar
½ cup (packed) brown sugar
pinch of salt
1 tbsp vanilla extract
3 cups hazelnuts, pecans, walnuts, brazil nuts or unsalted peanuts, or a combination
14 oz semi-sweet chocolate, chopped
2 tbsp white vegetable fat

semi-sweet chocolate

brazil nuts

walnuts

hazelnuts

peanuts

pecans

1 Lightly oil 2 cookie sheets with vegetable oil. In a large heavy-based saucepan over medium heat, cook the cream, butter, corn syrup, sugars and salt, stirring occasionally, until sugars dissolve and butter melts, about 3 minutes. Bring to a boil and continue cooking, stirring frequently, until caramel reaches 240°F (soft ball stage) on a sugar thermometer, about 1 hour.

2 Place bottom of saucepan into a pan of cold water to stop cooking or transfer caramel to a smaller saucepan. Cool slightly, then stir in vanilla.

3 Stir nuts into caramel until well-coated. Using an oiled tablespoon, drop tablespoonfuls of nut mixture on to prepared sheets, about 1 in apart. If mixture hardens, return to heat to soften. Refrigerate clusters for 30 minutes until firm and cold, or leave in a cool place until hardened.

4 Using a metal spatula, transfer clusters to a wire rack placed over a cookie sheet to catch drips. In a medium saucepan, over low heat, melt chocolate and white vegetable fat, stirring until smooth. Cool slightly.

5 Spoon chocolate over each cluster, being sure to cover completely. Alternatively, using a fork, dip each cluster into chocolate and lift out, tapping on edge of saucepan to shake off excess.

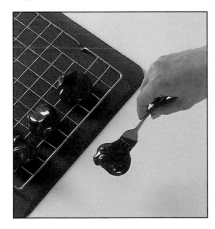

6 Place on a wire rack over a cookie sheet. Allow to set for 2 hours until hardened. Store in an airtight container.

Double Chocolate-Dipped Fruit

Just about any kind of fruit can be dipped in chocolate as long as the fruit is *dry*, because even one drop of moisture can cause the melted chocolate to seize and harden. To store chocolate-dipped fruit for more than 12 hours, the chocolate should be tempered.

Makes 24 coated pieces

INGREDIENTS

fruits – about 24 pieces (strawberries, cherries, orange segments, large seedless grapes, cape gooseberries, kumquats, pitted prunes, pitted dates, dried apricots, dried pears or nuts)

4 oz fine quality white chocolate, chopped

4 oz fine quality bittersweet or semi-sweet chocolate, chopped

cherries

grapes

cape gooseberries

strawberries

kumquats

dates

1 Clean and prepare fruits; wipe strawberries with a soft cloth or brush gently with pastry brush. Wash and dry firm-skinned fruits such as cherries and grapes; dry well and set on paper towels to absorb any remaining moisture. Peel or cut any other fruits being used. Dried or crystalized fruits can also be used.

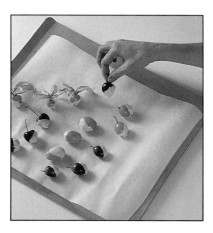

2 Melt white chocolate until smooth, stirring frequently. Remove from heat and cool to tepid (about 84°F), stirring frequently. Line a cookie sheet with waxed paper or parchment paper. Holding fruits by the stem or end and at an angle, dip about two-thirds of the fruit into the chocolate. Allow excess to drip off and place on cookie sheet. (If chocolate becomes too thick, set over hot water to soften slightly.) Refrigerate fruits until chocolate sets, about 20 minutes.

3 In the top of the cleaned double boiler over low heat, melt the bittersweet or semi-sweet chocolate, stirring frequently until smooth. Remove from heat and cool to just below body temperature, about 88°F.

4 Take each white chocolate-coated fruit from cookie sheet and, holding by the stem or end and at the opposite angle, dip bottom third of each piece into the dark chocolate, creating a chevron effect. Set on cookie sheet. Refrigerate for 15 minutes or until set. Remove from refrigerator 10–15 minutes before serving to soften chocolate.

Chocolate Christmas Cups

To crystalize cranberries for decoration, beat an egg white until frothy. Dip each berry first in the egg white then in superfine sugar. Place on sheets of waxed paper to dry.

Makes about 35 cups

INGREDIENTS
70–80 foil or paper candy cases
10 oz semi-sweet chocolate, broken
  into pieces
6 oz cooked, cold Christmas pudding
⅓ cup brandy or whisky
chocolate leaves and crystallized
  cranberries to decorate

semi-sweet chocolate

brandy

1 Place the chocolate in a medium bowl over a saucepan of hot water. Place saucepan over low heat until chocolate is melted, stirring frequently until chocolate is smooth. Using a pastry brush, brush or coat the bottom and side of about 35 candy cases. Allow to set, then repeat, reheating melted chocolate if necessary, applying a second coat. Leave to cool and set completely, 4–5 hours or overnight. Reserve remaining chocolate.

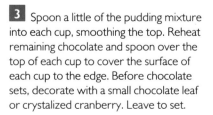

2 Crumble the Christmas pudding in a small bowl; sprinkle with brandy or whisky and allow to stand for 30–40 minutes, until brandy is absorbed.

3 Spoon a little of the pudding mixture into each cup, smoothing the top. Reheat remaining chocolate and spoon over the top of each cup to cover the surface of each cup to the edge. Before chocolate sets, decorate with a small chocolate leaf or crystalized cranberry. Leave to set.

4 When completely set, carefully peel off the cases and place in clean foil cases. Decorate with chocolate leaves and crystalized berries.

Chocolate Box with Caramel Mousse and Berries

Do not add caramel shards too long before serving the Chocolate Box as moisture may cause them to melt.

Serves 8–10

INGREDIENTS

10 oz semi-sweet chocolate, broken into pieces

CARAMEL MOUSSE
4 × 2 oz Heath bars, coarsely chopped
1½ tbsp milk or water
1½ cups heavy cream
1 egg white

CARAMEL SHARDS
½ cup granulated sugar
¼ cup water

TOPPING
4 oz fine quality white chocolate, chopped
1½ cups heavy cream
1 lb mixed berries or cut up fruits such as raspberries, strawberries, blackberries or sliced nectarine and orange segments

1 Prepare the chocolate box. Turn a 9 in square baking pan bottom-side up. Mold a piece of foil around the pan, then turn it right side up and line it with the foil, pressing against the edges to make the foil as smooth as possible.

2 Place the semi-sweet chocolate in a bowl over a saucepan of hot water. Place saucepan over low heat and stir until chocolate is melted and smooth. Immediately pour melted chocolate into the lined pan and tilt to coat bottom and sides evenly, keeping top edges of sides as straight as possible. As chocolate coats sides, tilt pan again to coat the corners and sides again. Refrigerate until firm, 45 minutes.

3 In a medium bowl, place the Heath bars and milk or water. Place over a pan of hot water over medium heat and stir until melted. Remove from heat and cool for 10 minutes, stirring occasionally. In a bowl with electric mixer, whip cream until soft peaks form. Stir a spoonful of cream into caramel mixture, then fold in remaining cream. In another bowl with electric mixer and cleaned beaters, beat egg white until just stiff; fold into mousse mixture. Pour into the box. Refrigerate for several hours or overnight.

semi-sweet chocolate

raspberries

chocolate bar

strawberries

eggs

white chocolate

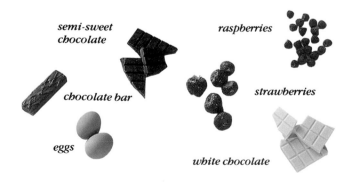

4 Meanwhile prepare the caramel shards. Lightly oil a cookie sheet. In a small saucepan over low heat, dissolve the sugar in the water, swirling pan gently. Increase the heat and boil mixture until sugar begins to turn a pale golden color, 4–5 minutes. When mixture is a golden caramel color, immediately pour on to the oiled sheet, tilt sheet to distribute caramel in an even layer; *do not touch — caramel is dangerously hot.* Cool completely, then using a metal spatula lift off cookie sheet and break into pieces. Set aside to decorate.

5 In a small saucepan over low heat, melt the white chocolate and ½ cup cream until smooth, stirring frequently. Strain into a medium bowl and cool to room temperature, stirring occasionally. In another bowl with electric mixer, beat the remaining cream until firm peaks form. Stir a spoonful of cream into the white chocolate mixture, then fold in remaining whipped cream. Using foil as a guide, remove mousse-filled box from the foil by peeling foil carefully from sides, then bottom. Slide on to serving plate.

6 Spoon chocolate-cream mixture into a medium piping bag fitted with a star tip and pipe a decorative design of rosettes or shells over the surface of the set mousse. Decorate the cream-covered box with the fruits and Caramel Shards.

Truffle-filled Easter Egg

This is a very fussy procedure, but the result is very rewarding and makes a welcome gift. The finished egg can be decorated with ribbons.

Makes 1 large, hollow Easter egg

INGREDIENTS
12 oz plain couverture chocolate, tempered, or plain, milk or white chocolate, melted
truffles (see Chocolate Truffles recipe)
melted chocolate

milk chocolate

plain chocolate

COOK'S TIP

To be sure there are no scratches or rough spots on the chocolate molds (this would cause chocolate to stick), use a cotton ball to polish the insides of two 6 in plastic Easter egg molds.

1 Line a small cookie sheet with waxed paper or parchment paper. Melt chocolate. Using a small ladle or spoon, pour in enough chocolate to coat the molds. Tilt the molds slowly to coat the sides completely; pour any excess back into the bowl of chocolate and set molds, open side down, on the prepared cookie sheet. Refrigerate for 1–2 minutes until just set.

   Apply second coat of chocolate and refrigerate for 1–3 minutes until set. Repeat a third time and refrigerate for at least 1 hour or until completely set. (Work quickly to avoid having to re-temper chocolate; untempered chocolate can be reheated if it hardens.)

2 To unmold eggs, trim any drops of chocolate from the edge of the mold. Gently insert the point of a small knife between the chocolate and the mold to break the air lock.

3 Holding the mold open side down, squeeze firmly to release the egg half. Repeat with the other half and refrigerate, loosely covered. (Do not touch chocolate surface with fingers as they will leave prints.) Reserve any melted chocolate to reheat for 'glue'.

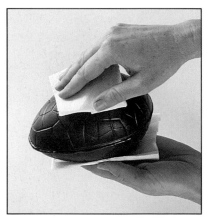

4 To assemble the egg, hold one half of the egg with a piece of folded paper towel or foil and fill with small truffles. If necessary use the remaining melted chocolate to use as 'glue'. Spread a small amount on to the rim of the egg half and, holding the empty egg half with a piece of paper towel or foil, press it on to the filled half, making sure the rims are carefully joined.

5 Hold for several seconds, then prop up egg with the folded paper towel or foil and refrigerate to set. If you like, decorate the egg with ribbons or Easter decorations.

White Chocolate Celebration Cake

The ingredients for the white chocolate cake make one 12 in layer, therefore you will need double the ingredients for the cake and buttercream, preparing each batch separately to ensure even baking. If you wish to make a smaller cake, bake only one layer and split and fill with one quantity of buttercream and half quantities of lemon syrup and lemon curd.

Serves 40–50

INGREDIENTS
4 cups flour
2 tsp baking soda
pinch of salt
8 oz white chocolate, chopped
1 cup whipping cream
1 cup unsalted butter, softened
2 cups superfine sugar
6 eggs
2 tsp lemon extract
grated zest of 1 lemon
1⅓ cups buttermilk
chocolate leaves to decorate

LEMON SYRUP
½ cup granulated sugar
½ cup water
2 tbsp fresh lemon juice

WHITE CHOCOLATE CREAM CHEESE BUTTER CREAM
12 oz white chocolate, chopped
18 oz cream cheese, softened
1¼ cup unsalted butter, at room temperature
2 tbsp fresh lemon juice
½ tsp lemon extract

LEMON CURD
Follow the recipe on page 42. You will need double the quantity.

4–8 tbsp unsalted butter, softened, or margarine, for spreading

COOK'S TIP
When beating in eggs, if mixture appears to curdle, sprinkle over a little flour mixture to bind.

eggs

lemons

fresh flowers

white chocolate

white chocolate leaves

1 Prepare cake layers. Preheat oven to 350°F. Grease a 12 in cake pan or springform pan. Line bottom with waxed paper or parchment paper, grease again, then flour lightly.

Into a bowl, sift together flour, baking soda and salt, set aside. In a saucepan over medium heat, melt chocolate and cream, stirring until smooth. Set aside to cool.

In a bowl with electric mixer, beat the butter until creamy, then add sugar and beat for 2–3 minutes. Beat in eggs one at a time, beating well after each addition.

Slowly beat in melted chocolate, lemon extract and zest. Alternately, on low speed, add flour in 4 batches and buttermilk in 3 batches, until batter is smooth. Pour into pan. Bake for 1 hour or until cake tester comes out clean. If top browns before center is cooked, cover with foil.

Remove cake to rack to cool for 10 minutes. Invert cake on to rack and cool completely. When cool, wrap in plastic wrap until ready to assemble. Make second cake in the same way.

2 Prepare syrup. In a small saucepan, combine sugar and water. Over medium heat bring to a boil, stirring until sugar dissolves. Remove from heat, stir in lemon juice and cool completely. Store in an airtight container. Prepare the lemon curd as instructed on page 42, and cover with clear film.

3 Prepare butter cream. Place chocolate in a bowl over a pan of hot water over low heat and stir until melted. (Do not allow chocolate to become too hot, remove from heat if necessary, then return for further melting.) Cool slightly. In a bowl with electric mixer, beat cream cheese until smooth. Gradually beat in cooled white chocolate, then butter, lemon juice and extract. Refrigerate until ready to use.

4 To assemble, split each cake in half. Spoon syrup over each layer, allowing it to soak in, then repeat. Spread bottom half of each cake with lemon curd and replace top layers. Gently beat butter cream until creamy. Spread a quarter over the top of one of the filled cakes. Place the second filled cake on top. Spread a small amount of softened butter over top and sides to create a smooth, crumb-free surface. Refrigerate for 30 minutes to set.

5 Place cake on serving plate. Reserving a quarter of the butter cream for piping, spread remaining butter cream over top and sides of the cake. Spoon reserved butter cream into a large piping bag fitted with a star tip and pipe a shell pattern around edges of the cake. Decorate with chocolate leaves and fresh flowers.

Chocolate Christmas Log

Begin preparations for this cake at least one day ahead. It is easy to prepare, but has several components. Make the mushrooms by sandwiching small meringues together with ganache.

Serves 12–14

INGREDIENTS
5 eggs, separated
3 tbsp cocoa plus extra for dusting
⅛ tsp cream of tartar
1 cup confectioners' sugar

CHOCOLATE GANACHE FROSTING
1¼ cups heavy or whipping cream
12 oz bittersweet chocolate, chopped
2 tbsp brandy or chocolate-flavor liqueur

CRANBERRY CHRISTMAS SAUCE
1 lb fresh or frozen cranberries, rinsed and picked over
1 cup seedless raspberry preserve, melted
½ cup granulated sugar, or to taste

WHITE CHOCOLATE CREAM FILLING
7 oz fine quality white chocolate, chopped
2 cups heavy cream
2 tbsp brandy or chocolate-flavor liqueur (optional)

raspberry preserve

bittersweet chocolate

cranberries

COOK'S TIP
Small decorative 'mushrooms' are traditionally used to enhance the chocolate yule log. These can be made from meringue. Pipe the 'caps' and 'stems' separately, and when dry and hard, stick together using a little ganache or melted chocolate. You may lightly dust them with cocoa after assembling.

1 Prepare frosting. In a medium saucepan over medium heat, bring the cream to a boil. Remove from heat and add chocolate all at once, stirring constantly until melted and smooth. Stir in liqueur if using, then strain into a medium bowl and cool to room temperature. Remove ½ cup at room temperature, refrigerate remaining ganache for 6–8 hours or overnight.

3 Prepare cake. Preheat oven to 400°F. Grease 15½ × 10½ in jelly roll pan, line with greased waxed paper or parchment paper, overlapping edge.

In a bowl with electric mixer, beat yolks until thick and creamy. Reduce speed and beat in cocoa and half the sugar. In large bowl with electric mixer with cleaned beaters, beat egg whites. Add cream of tartar and beat on high speed until soft peaks form. Add remaining sugar 2 tbsp at a time, beating well after each addition until stiff and glossy. Gently fold beaten yolk mixture into the whites. Spread batter in pan and bake for 15–20 minutes.

Lay a clean dish towel on a work surface and cover with waxed paper or parchment paper; dust with cocoa or sugar. When cake is done, immediately turn out on to paper. Peel off lining paper. Cut off crisp edges and, starting from one narrow end, roll cake with the paper and towel, jelly roll fashion. Cool cake, seam side down, on rack.

2 Prepare sauce. In a food processor fitted with a metal blade, process the cranberries until liquid. Press through a sieve into a small bowl, discard pulp. Stir in melted raspberry preserve and sugar to taste. If sauce is too thick, add a little water to thin. Refrigerate until ready to serve.

4 Prepare filling. In a saucepan over low heat, melt white chocolate with ½ cup cream until melted, stirring frequently. Strain into a bowl and cool to room temperature. In another bowl with electric mixer, beat remaining cream and brandy until soft peaks form. Stir a spoonful of cream into white chocolate mixture to lighten it, then fold in remaining cream. Unroll cooled cake and spread with chocolate cream. Starting from the same end, reroll cake. Cut off one-quarter of the cake at an angle. Place against the long piece to resemble a branch.

5 Allow frosting to soften at room temperature. With an electric mixer, beat the ganache until it begins to lighten in color and texture, about 30–45 seconds. It should have a soft spreading consistency; do not over-beat as chocolate will become stiff and grainy. Using a metal spatula, spread ganache over the cake surface. Using a fork, mark the ganache lengthwise to resemble tree bark. Dust cake with confectioners' sugar and serve with cranberry sauce.

Death by Chocolate

There are many versions of this cake; this is a very rich one which is ideal for a large party, as it can serve up to twenty chocolate lovers.

Serves 18–20

INGREDIENTS
8 oz fine quality bittersweet
    chocolate, chopped
½ cup unsalted butter, cut into pieces
⅔ cup water
1¼ cups granulated sugar
2 tsp vanilla extract
2 eggs, separated
⅔ cup buttermilk or sour cream
2 cups flour
2 tsp baking powder
1 tsp baking soda
pinch of cream of tartar
chocolate curls
raspberries and confectioners' sugar
    to decorate (optional)

CHOCOLATE FUDGE FILLING
1 lb fine quality couverture chocolate
    or bittersweet chocolate, chopped
1 cup unsalted butter
⅓ cup brandy or rum
¾ cup seedless raspberry preserve

CHOCOLATE GANACHE GLAZE
1 cup heavy cream
8 oz couverture chocolate or
    bittersweet chocolate, chopped
2 tbsp brandy

1 Preheat oven to 350°F. Grease a 10 in springform pan and line base with parchment paper or waxed paper. In a saucepan over medium-low heat, heat chocolate, butter and water until melted, stirring frequently. Remove from heat, beat in sugar and vanilla and cool.

In a bowl, beat yolks lightly, then beat into cooled chocolate mixture; gently fold in buttermilk or sour cream. Into a bowl, sift flour, baking powder and baking soda, then fold into chocolate mixture. In a bowl with an electric mixer, beat egg whites and cream of tartar until stiff peaks form; fold in chocolate mixture.

2 Pour mixture into prepared pans and bake for 45–50 minutes until cake begins to shrink away from side of pan. Remove to a wire rack to cool for 10 minutes (cake may sink in center, this is normal). Run a sharp knife around the edge of pan, then unclip pan and carefully remove side. Invert cake on to wire rack, remove bottom of pan and cool completely. Wash and dry pan.

3 Prepare filling. In a saucepan over medium heat, heat chocolate, butter and 4 tbsp brandy until melted, stirring frequently. Remove from heat and set aside to cool and thicken. Cut cake crosswise into three even layers. Heat the raspberry preserve and remaining brandy until melted and smooth, stirring frequently. Spread a thin layer over each of the cake layers and allow to set.

4 When the filling is spreadable, place the bottom cake layer back in the pan. Spread with half the filling, top with the second layer of cake, then spread with the remaining filling and top with the top cake layer, preserve side down. Gently press layers together, cover and refrigerate for 4–6 hours or overnight.

bittersweet chocolate

eggs

chocolate curls

raspberries

5 Carefully run a sharp knife around edge of cake to loosen, then unclip and remove side of pan. Set cake on wire rack over a cookie sheet to catch any drips. In a medium saucepan, bring the cream to a boil. Remove from heat and add chocolate all at once, stirring until melted and smooth. Stir in the brandy and strain into a bowl. Allow to stand for 4–5 minutes to thicken slightly.

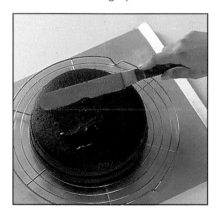

6 Beginning from the center of the bowl and working out towards the edge, whisk the glaze until smooth and shiny. Pour over the cake using a metal spatula to help smooth top and sides; allow glaze to set. Slide cake on to serving plate and decorate with chocolate curls and raspberries. Dust with confectioners' sugar. Do not refrigerate glaze or it will become dull.

INDEX